THE FATHER'S GIFT

THE FATHER'S GIFT
Discovering What Every Believer Receives in Christ
S. Lloyd Walters

Published by:
SCEPTER COMMUNICATIONS, INC.
A Division of AMI INC.
Post Office Box 160781 | Altamonte Springs, FL 32716-0781
www.amiintl.org

All rights reserved. No part of this book may be reproduced or transmitted in any form or by any means, electronic or mechanical, including photocopying, recording, or by any information storage and retrieval system, without written permission from the author, except for the inclusion of brief quotations in a review. For information, please contact the publisher.

Copyright © 2007-2013 by S. Lloyd Walters
All Rights Reserved.

ISBN 10: 0983546401
ISBN 13: 978-0-9835464-0-5

Library of Congress Control Number: 2012903713

Cover Design:
Sehon Glynn / SGraphixs
www.sgraphixs.com

Cover & Interior Layout:
Kathleen Schubitz / RPJ & Company, Inc.
www.rpjandco1417.com

Scriptures taken from the Holy Bible, New International Version®, NIV®. Copyright © 1973, 1978, 1984, 2011 by Biblica, Inc.™ Used by permission of Zondervan. All rights reserved worldwide.www.zondervan.com.

Scripture verses identified as KJV are from the *King James Version* of the Bible.

Printed in the United States of America

To Sean and Camille, for your sacrifice and unconditional love

To my "baby sister" Andrea
and all brand new believers just like you

Table of Contents

S. LLOYD WALTERS

Published by
Scepter Communications, Inc.
A Division of AMI Inc.
Altamonte Springs, Florida

ACKNOWLEDGMENTS

Special thanks to Sharon Williams of Docufit Graphics for her invaluable contribution toward and her tutelage regarding publishing.

Special thanks to my mom, Olive Walters, for her tolerance and patience as this work was birthed in the solitude and isolation of her Altamonte Springs, Florida home.

Special thanks also to Cherlane Harris whose obedience to the Spirit of God converted a hand-written manuscript into a digital format.

Preface

A well known singer (who will remain nameless) was getting married. She stated on national television that she had to get a videotape of a wedding to see how it was done. The reason for that was she had never been to a church or seen a church wedding.

She represents a huge segment of American society today: young adults and their children who have never been to a church and know little of its language or traditions. Some may have attended as children, but all that is retained are phrases and clichés that have little meaning or are barely understood.

This led to the preparation of a teaching tool that could be used in ministry to explain to seekers and new believers the basics of Christianity. This tool was to be written so that it would be understandable to anyone without regard to the level of exposure to religion and its jargon or rituals.

Early on in the preparation stage of the booklet, preliminarily called *Basic Training,* I entered into my own crisis of faith. I had recently been led to leave the denomination in which I was born and of which my mother's family had been members for three generations. All of my immediate family, aunts, uncles and cousins were lifelong members as well. I had been taught in its schools from the first grade through graduate school, grew up in its youth organizations, and finally, to the pride and delight of my entire family, was trained and ordained as a pastor. Now I was directed by the Spirit of God to leave everything that took decades to build.

This uprooting included upheaval in my personal life. Evidently I would have to lose my life in order to find it.[1] The instructions I received required me to embark on this journey alone.

Obviously, this was a major crisis for me, not only personally, but also for my faith in all that I had been taught and preached to others for years. Was the church of my grandfather and mother somehow out of step with the scriptures? Or had I been subtly deceived and was listening to the wrong voice? I had to find the truth. It was not as if I were perfect and flawless in my own life, yet I wanted to make sure that I was on the path that led to life and the destiny that God had for me.[2]

For months I prayed, fasted and diligently searched the scriptures for answers. I was a seminary trained theologian, but that did not help. I grew up in the church, but that also was of no assistance. Gradually each day the Spirit of God revealed His will and answered each of my questions. Each revelation was confirmed in His word. He taught me in ways that astounded me. In the process of guiding me in the new direction of my life and ministry, God also clarified the basic and essential elements of Christianity.

Out of the travail of these circumstances God birthed this work. It is a revelation that instructed and comforted a troubled and questioning preacher with the gospel that is seldom preached or taught so that it could be widely understood. This reveals the ultimate purpose of this book: To share and teach about the awesome Gift that the Father has freely given to every believer.

---

[1] See Matthew 16:25, Mark 8:35 and Luke 9:25

[2] The complete story will be told in a future autobiographical work preliminarily entitled, No More Lies

THE FATHER'S GIFT

Chapter 1

INTRODUCTION

The Pharisees heard that Jesus was gaining and baptizing more disciples than John, although in fact it was not Jesus who baptized, but his disciples. When the Lord learned of this, he left Judea and went back once more to Galilee. Now he had to go through Samaria. So he came to a town in Samaria called Sychar, near the plot of ground Jacob had given to his son Joseph. Jacob's well was there, and Jesus, tired as he was from the journey, sat down by the well. It was about the sixth hour. When a Samaritan woman came to draw water, Jesus said to her, "Will you give me a drink?" (His disciples had gone into the town to buy food.) The Samaritan woman said to him, "You are a Jew and I am a Samaritan woman. How can you ask me for a drink?" (For Jews do not associate with Samaritans.) Jesus answered her, "If you knew the gift of God and who it is that asks you for a drink, you would have asked him and he would have given you living water" (John 4:1-10).

For God so loved the world that he gave his one and only Son, that whoever believes in him shall not perish but have eternal life. For God did not send his Son into the world to condemn the world, but to save the world through him (John 3:16-17).

But because of his great love for us, God, who is rich in mercy, made us alive with Christ even when we were dead in transgressions—it is by grace you have been saved. And God raised us up with Christ and seated us with him in the heavenly realms in Christ Jesus, in order that in the coming ages he might show the incomparable riches of his grace, expressed in his kindness to us in Christ Jesus. For it is by grace you have been saved, through faith—and this not from yourselves, it is the gift of God—not by works, so that no one can boast (Ephesians 2:4-9).

Thanks be to God for his indescribable gift! (2 Corinthians 9:15).

All of us at some time in our lives have received gifts. Whether for Christmas or our birthdays, it is always a joy to receive something special from someone else. Unfortunately some gifts, though well intended, may end up in a closet (or worse) within a short period of time.

Then, of course, there are those gifts that stand out. It might have come from someone special. The gift itself might have been well thought out and expensive. Each time you look at it or think about it the appreciation and gratitude both for the giver and the gift grows and warms the heart. It is this kind of gift that one would probably boast about to one's friends or share with anyone who would care to hear what it felt like to receive such generosity and kindness.

This characterizes, in part, the motivation for writing this book. Added to that is the fact that the Gift discussed here is not just for one person, but it is available to anyone who is willing to receive it.

Perhaps you were never told about the Gift offered to you by God, our Father. It may have been explained in a way that you didn't get a clear understanding of what believers actually receive from God. Perhaps it seemed so complicated or had so many conditions attached to it that it no longer seemed like a gift anymore. You may have a vague understanding of the Gift from God, but would like to look a little closer and deeper into the subject. You might just simply be curious about Christianity or want a deeper and clearer grasp of the subject. If these or other reasons prompted you to examine these pages, this book, then, is for you.

One gift with many wonderful and unbelievable benefits

In the Word of God, a Gift is offered to every man, woman, boy and girl who ever lived or will ever live on this planet. This Gift is so amazing that Paul borrows from Habakkuk and says "you would never believe it even if someone told you."[1] Jesus talked about it in His conversation with the Samaritan woman at Jacob's well. He said it would become a spring of water in a person welling up to eternal life.

Notice that it is referred to as a gift. It is not earned, worked for or related in any way to some thing that was done in exchange for it. It is a singular gift. It is one gift with many wonderful and unbelievable benefits.

Each chapter of this book will explore one specific aspect of God's Gift. Each problem created by man's rebellion against God is examined, how that problem was solved and how the solution applies to each believer in a practical way. The first chapter will establish the foundation of everything that will follow. Like the construction of a building where the concrete footings are put securely in place so that the structure to come can be supported, the first step in this process is to establish the fundamental elements necessary so that what follows can stand and be understood.

Each chapter will address a specific non-negotiable issue that God determined had to be handled in the believer's favor and then was freely offered as a gift to those who would receive it. Those issues include being His mortal enemy, the sentence of death hanging over our collective heads, being born in the wrong family, having an evil nature and how to get that believer into a better family and a new nature. The last chapter explores what one's response to all of this will be.

Each chapter begins with the primary portions of the Word of God alluded to within. In some instances the portions of scriptures will be long. The reason for this is because in many of the writings of the Bible, especially in the New Testament, the books were actually letters that were written by the Apostles. Even for those that were not

[1] In Acts 13:41 Paul is writing to Jews who were well versed in the scriptures, yet he suggests that the gospel about Christ Jesus would be hard to believe.

letters, when one simply lifts a sentence or two out of its context, one might miss the point that the original writer was making. Every effort will be made to be consistent with the intent of the original writer.

Also, at the end of each chapter are endnotes, most of which are scripture references. The reader is encouraged to take some time to look up these texts because they will shed more light on the points made in each chapter.

The Only Source: The Bible

The only source for this book is the Bible. It is generally accepted as the most authoritative revelation of God to man. Prophets and their prophecies are tested by it.[2] Every human experience or practice, whether ordinary or supernatural is judged valid or invalid based on its teachings.[3] Therefore, the written Word of God will be cited exclusively and exhaustively in the pages of this book.

This subject was never meant to be so confusing that only professional theologians could understand it. Every effort will be made to make it easy to understand by the widest possible audience. Some terms freely tossed around in religious circles will be explained, hopefully, in a way that the average reader will be able to comprehend what is being said. The gospel is meant for everyone, so until everyone has an opportunity to at least hear and understand it, we, who are commissioned to spread this good news (which is what the word "gospel" means), have not completed our task.

The Gift is the doorway, highway, vehicle and the destination all at the same time

[2] Isaiah 8:19-20

[3] 2 Timothy 3:16-17

This work is not the first word on this subject and is by no means the last. It is simply a starting point. The closer we look at this Gift, the more there is to see. The deeper we dig, the more treasure we find. Paul refers to this as "unsearchable riches."

Many of us know John 3:16 by memory. It states that God so loved the world that He gave his only begotten Son. There is something, however, that is taken for granted. Many have taken that as a text about being saved. A closer look will point out that God gave His Son. That might seem simple enough, but what does His giving His Son entitle believers to?

Human beings are inherent legalists

For many, this is either avoiding hell or making it to heaven. These considerations, while of paramount importance, are only a small portion of what is available through God's Gift. Some might argue it is about eternal life. That is also true, but there is even more than that available to every believer right now.

There are others who might suggest that it is prosperity as measured by material wealth, such as expensive cars, large homes and bank accounts that God is anxious to bring everyone's way. Without suggesting that God's favor may be manifested in intangible and material ways, that is not His primary purpose.[4] In fact, many of those who first learned of and taught others about this Gift were destitute of this world's goods and "content with just food and clothing."[5]

The Gift that God has given to us is the doorway, highway, vehicle and the destination all at the same time. It is our great reward. It is our inheritance. It is our peace, our salvation, our healing, our deliverance, our righteousness, our sanctification, our justification and our glory. It is both our death and our life.

---

[4] See 2 Timothy 6:3-10, Philippians 4:10-13, 2 Corinthians 6:3-10, 1 Corinthians 4:8-13 and Hebrews 11:32-40

[5] 1 Timothy 6:8

It however, is not an "it." It is not a thing. It is not a building, a temple or a place. It is a He. God the Father gave us His Son. "Today in the town of David has been born to you; he is Christ the Lord."[6] Of Himself, Jesus said that He is the Good Shepherd, the door, the bread, the living water, the truth, the resurrection and the life. No one has access to the Father (where every good gift comes from)[7] except by and through Him.

For many, the gospel is about escaping the fires of Hell, living a morally upright life, going to church or "getting my stuff." In other words, it is about us. However, in Romans 1:1-6, Paul describes the gospel as the gospel of God regarding His Son. The benefits received through Him are not because of us even though we are the beneficiaries. God has done all of these things for the sake of His name. The name Jesus means "Jehovah Saves" or "Jehovah is a Savior." He was living up to His name. He is the author and finisher of our faith, the Alpha and Omega (the first and last letters of the Greek alphabet). He is all and in all. And God gave Him as a Gift to us; to all of us. The gospel then, is not about us, but about Him.

One key point; He is a Gift. Why then is there such a struggle to earn, attain or possess something that is freely given? One reason is the human tendency to believe that no one gives anyone something for nothing, especially something of great value. This is the foundation of legalism. That is why Paul suggested that many would have difficulty believing it. Human beings are inherent legalists. They develop an intense sense of right and wrong, along with a penalty for violating that code of conduct (whatever it may be based upon). Children call it fairness. Adults call it justice.

The gospel however is not fair or just from a legalistic point of view. The innocent suffered for the guilty and the

---

[6] Luke 2:11

[7] James 1:17

guilty are set free. That is unfair and unjust, yet it pleased the Lord to bruise Him.[8] That is difficult to internalize for most "fair minded" people.

Another reason for this legalism is because the language of the old Sinai covenant and the prophecies cited by Jesus and the apostles are found in the same writings: the Old Testament. This is where they discovered the concepts, elements, principles and scriptures that the New Testament writers used to put their faith in Jesus. Contained in those same scriptures is the legalistic language and concepts of the old covenant (the Ten Commandments). There is much to be learned by the events, circumstances and the teachings of the old covenant. However, as the writer of Hebrews put it, if the old covenant were sufficient there would be no need for the new.[9] John puts it this way, "The law came through Moses, but grace and truth came through Jesus Christ."[10] This will be explored in greater detail in the next chapter.

Jesus himself told a group of Hebrew scholars and leaders that they diligently study the scriptures and think that by them they possess eternal life, yet these (the scriptures) are they that testify of Him. Yet they persistently refused to come to Him to receive life.[11] In other words, they (the scribes and Pharisees) diligently investigated the scriptures yet missed the central message and the whole point. He was, is and always will be the central theme and the most vital point of the scriptures.

Today many religious people, churches, institutions and denominations pile on top of unsuspecting seekers and believers layers and layers of conditions, requirements and do's and don't's as conditions to receiving and/or keeping the Gift freely offered by God. In many ways this situation parallels the environment in Jesus' time.

[8] Isaiah 53:10

[9] Hebrews 7:11, 18; 8:7, 13; 9:8

[10] John 1:17

[11] John 5:39-40

Many early believers exchanged allegiances to generations-old religious tradition, creeds, and organizations, long held doctrinal positions, loss of income and cherished personal or family relationships were willingly forfeited for this wonderful Gift proclaimed by the apostles and taught to untold thousands of others. Since then, through the writings of these same apostles, many have believed their report and testimony. Even the threat of loss of life itself has not been a deterrent to receiving this wonderful Gift.

The Gift that God has given us in Christ is the substance of the gospel, the meaning of all of the sacrifices of bulls, lambs, goats and other animals in the Jewish temple system and totality of the message of the apostles. As Paul wrote to the believers in Corinth some teaching and principles about giving and generosity, he was reminded about God's generosity in giving the Gift of His Son and exclaimed in the middle of his letter, "thanks be to God for His indescribable Gift!" As you read the pages of this book, may that be your sentiment as well.

Chapter 2

Foundations

For God so loved the world that he gave his one and only Son, that whoever believes in him shall not perish but have eternal life. For God did not send his Son into the world to condemn the world, but to save the world through him. Whoever believes in him is not condemned, but whoever does not believe stands condemned already because he has not believed in the name of God's one and only Son (John 3:16-18).

For it is by grace you have been saved, through faith—and this not from yourselves, it is the gift of God—not by works, so that no one can boast (Ephesians 2:8-9).

For in Christ Jesus neither circumcision nor uncircumcision has any value. The only thing that counts is faith expressing itself through love (Galatians 5:6).

But the man who has doubts is condemned if he eats, because his eating is not from faith; and everything that does not come from faith is sin (Romans 14:23).

I am not ashamed of the gospel, because it is the power of God for the salvation of everyone who believes: first for the Jew, then for the Gentile. For in the gospel a righteousness from God is revealed, a righteousness that is by faith from first to last, just as it is written: "The righteous will live by faith" (Romans 1:16-17).

Now faith is being sure of what we hope for and certain of what we do not see. And without faith it is impossible to please God, because anyone who comes to him must believe that he exists and that he rewards those who earnestly seek him (Hebrews 11:1, 6).

The most essential foundational element necessary to understanding how to acquire this Gift offered by God is faith. There are many views on this subject and there will be many others. However, for the purposes of this discussion, an examination of the biblical definition would be helpful.

Faith

Faith, the Bible says, comes by hearing and hearing by the Word of God.[1] In other words, faith begins with and is based on the written Word of God. There are two words in the Greek language translated "word": *logos* and *rhema*. Allow me to suggest that a *logos* word represents the written scriptures found in the sixty-six books of the Bible and a *rhema* word is a divine communication one receives by unction from the Spirit of God, prophecy from the mouth of a prophet or direct revelation by a vision or a dream.[2] The *logos* word is universal and general, while the *rhema* word is limited and specific to a small group or even to one individual.[3]

Faith is not wishful thinking or optimism. It is not visualizing what one wants. Faith works like this: God

---

[1] Romans 10:17 (KJV); Hebrews 4:12-13 The Hebrews passage, while is is generally attributed to the written word of God, introduces some aspects that might more specifically apply to the living Word of God embodied in the person of Christ Jesus as He is referred to in John 1:1-14 and Revelation 19:13

[2] In the New Testament Paul discusses the gifts of prophecy and word of knowledge. There are also the offices of pastor, teacher and evangelist as well as those of prophet and apostle. Throughout the book of Acts there are references to prophets and apostles other than the original twelve (Acts 11:27-28, 13:1, 14:14, 15:32, 21:10-14). The Corinthian believers were encouraged to especially desire the gift of prophecy (1 Corinthians 14:39). The testimony of Jesus is the spirit of prophecy (Revelation 19:10) and He is still testifying today corporately and individually. If the offices of pastor, teacher and evangelist are functioning in and continue to be important to the body of Christ today, the apostle and the prophet continue to as well.

[3] Dr. Bill Hamon is to be credited with shedding enormous light on his subject in Prophets and Personal Prophecy (1987), The Prophetic Movement (1990) and Prophets, Pitfalls and Principles (1991) Destiny Image New Kensington, PA.

makes a statement, one believes it, and then the believer walks and acts on the basis of what God has spoken. Centuries ago there had never been rain on the earth, yet God told a man to build a boat because not only was it going to rain, but it would rain so much that every living creature will be destroyed in the upcoming flood.[4] When the man began to chop down trees and warn his friends and neighbors of what God had revealed to him, he was operating by faith.

An angel appeared at a young woman's house who was engaged to be married and told her she would have a child. She was a virgin. She had not had sex with a man before. Yet, her response simply was: "be it unto me according to your word."[5] Faith is enduring, with joy, the ridicule and embarrassment of the whispers of neighbors and onlookers as this young unmarried woman carried the unborn Christ to term because God asked that of her.

Faith is an affirmative and active response to something God has said

Faith is going to battle, at the command of God against 135,000 battle-tested soldiers, with 300 men; and expecting to win![6]

Notice in each case, (and there are thousands more), faith begins with God's statement or word. In each instance, the thing God said defied human logic, or simply did not make sense. It was unexpected, unconventional, and often opened one up to ridicule, embarrassment and even criticism.

Faith then believes God's declarations to the extent that nothing is allowed to shake one's confidence in the word spoken by God. Put another way, faith is an affirmative and

[4] Genesis 6:1-9:17
[5] Luke 1:38 (KJV)
[6] See Judges 7

active response to something God has said. There are many things that will attempt to shake one from God's word. Friends or family can, at times, pressure you. A contrary word from a trusted teacher, doctor, or, even a preacher on a cd or in a pulpit can sometimes challenge one's faith. The traditions of religion often create barriers to faith in God's Word. One's own doubts and the pressures of everyday life can test your perseverance and resolve.

Doubts and fears are the killers of faith

The writer of Hebrews wrote, "Without faith it is impossible to please God, because anyone who comes to Him must believe that He exists and that He rewards those who earnestly seek Him."[7] After hearing the word, one must believe it. That sounds easy, but God asks us to believe things that contradict the norm, our traditions, our comfort zone, our feelings and what everybody else thinks. Sometimes, to believe the word God has spoken causes the believer to stand alone.

This raises an important point. Faith is not based on anything other than God's word. It is not based on popularly held views no matter how wide spread or who promotes it. Many base their faith on statements and sayings made in a service, crusade, conference or on television by local or national ministries without prayerfully examining the word for themselves and confirming that the word alluded to is God's specific will for them. Gideon won a war with only 300 men, but don't assume that you can get a few hundred of your buddies together and engage our latest national enemy however vile and evil they may be.

The issue is not watching television ministries or attending conferences. There are many great men and women of God ministering on television and conducting powerfully spiritual conferences around the world and

[7] Hebrews 11:6

delivering the word to millions. It is, however, about carefully and prayerfully examining whether the word is from God and if it is for that specific believer. The Berean believers were commended because they searched the scriptures to determine if what Paul, the most prolific writer of the New Testament, presented was so or not.[8]

There is a very important principle in the scriptures that states that every word, including rhema words, must be confirmed with two or three witnesses.[9] Even Jesus yielded to that principle when addressing the scribes and Pharisees in debate.[10] When challenged by Satan in the wilderness He resorted, again to the logos word[11], the sword of the Spirit,[12] as His primary weapon against the enemy. God will confirm His word, especially major life changing instruction, with multiple confirmations, often including scripture.

The believer's faith is grounded fully on the Word of God. This is what the classical definition of faith found in Hebrews 11:1 is referring to when it says that faith is the substance of things hoped for and the evidence of things not seen. What is hoped for is the thing promised by God and faith sees it before it becomes a reality.

Many times God states things that have yet to happen as if they already had taken place. He speaks things that are not as though they are.[13] When the angel of the Lord approached Gideon for the first time, he referred to him as "mighty warrior."[14] Gideon had fought no battles nor won any wars. In fact, he was hiding in a winepress threshing wheat. Yet God, who is not limited by time or space, spoke about his future as if it had already taken place.

---

[8] Acts 17:11

[9] See Deuteronomy 19:15 and 2 Corinthians 13:1

[10] John 5:31-47

[11] Matthew 4:1-11 and Luke 4:1-13

[12] Ephesians 6:17

[13] Romans 4:17

[14] Judges 6:12

When Joshua encountered the Man at Jericho who was later identified as the Commander of the Lord's hosts, He stated, "I have delivered Jericho into your hands." The Israelites had not marched around Jericho one time yet, but God spoke as if the battle was already over and the victory won.[15]

He spoke His word to Mary and nine months later Jesus was born. Yet, when He spoke to Abraham, it took twenty-five years before Isaac, his promised son, was born. In both instances His word came to pass. For Mary it happened in a short time, but for Abraham, there were a significant number of years between the word and its realization. Both the word and the timing of the fulfillment of that word are in God's control, so faith also requires patience to wait on God's timing and trust that He will fulfill His promises.

Faith is not wishful thinking or optimism

Many are too impatient to wait on God, and this is where many struggle and fail. Waiting, as mentioned before, is difficult, but essential when it comes to faith.

Receiving

After believing the word, Jesus used a term in Mark 11:20-24 that is another necessary element of faith: receiving. Believing involves mentally understanding and grasping the concepts spoken by God. Many hear and believe the word. James says that the devils believe,[16] but receiving takes the believer to another level.[17] When one has received the word it affects their walk and talk, even before the manifestation of what is promised.

---

[15] Joshua 5:13-6:2
[16] James 2:19
[17] Mark 11:20-25

A blind man named Bartimaeus was sitting at the city gate begging for money. When he realized that Jesus was passing by, he began to shout to enlist Jesus' help. People began to be annoyed at the commotion that he was making and told him to be quiet. His response was to shout louder. This, from his perspective, was a chance to see again and he would not miss his opportunity. When Jesus stopped and sent for him, Bartimaeus did something significant: he threw his cloak aside. In those days blind people were identified by a specific kind of cloak that they would wear so that others could see it and recognize that the person was blind. When Jesus responded to his cries for help and mercy, he threw his cloak aside as if to say, "I won't be needing this anymore." Even though he had not yet obtained his sight, he received it by faith. In fact, Jesus refers to his actions of shouting, persisting and throwing his cloak aside as faith.[18]

Receiving means that the believer places so much trust in the Word that his language and actions are affected more by it than his circumstances, situation or surroundings. Paul says, "I believed therefore I have spoken. With that same spirit of faith we also believe and therefore speak."[19]

As the Israelites were entering Canaan, they had to step into the water before it parted and then they crossed on the dry riverbed.[20] Their belief in God's word was received and translated into their actions. King Jehosophat, facing an invasion force of three combined kingdoms, received the word that they would not even have to fight the battle. A prophet revealed that God would defeat their enemies Himself. The king then organized the musicians and singers. They began to celebrate the victory before the battle even began. The Bible states that as they began to sing and to praise, the Lord went into action on their behalf. King Jehosophat

[18] Mark 10:46-52

[19] 2 Corinthians 4:13

[20] Joshua 3:14-17

received the word with joy, thanksgiving and praise. This is an expression of faith in the word and as a result he experienced the victory before the battle was actually won.[21]

From a human point of view this can be risky. It requires courage: courage to stand when others bow; courage to leave when others say stay; courage to stay on course when pressures are mounting to go another way; courage to stand alone.

Also, one's faith will be tested, not only by the enemy, but by God. Many great men of God were placed in extreme and trying circumstances to test them. This is what is known as the wilderness walk. Moses had his. David had his. Paul had his. Jesus had his. Moses, understanding the ways of God, told Israel that God lead them in the desert to humble and to test them in order to know what was in their hearts.[22] The word promised by God will be challenged by negative circumstances, problems, difficulties, apparent delays, competing pressures and interests, questions raised by others and sometimes by seemingly conflicting commands by God.

Abraham's promise of innumerable descendants was challenged by God's subsequent command to sacrifice the child of the promise, Isaac. With tears in his heart, but an unwavering faith in God's promise, Abraham proceeded, and obeyed the command believing that somehow God's promise would somehow still come to pass. True to His word, God provided a solution that did not affect His promises to him. But that did not come before a heart-wrenching, three day journey to the mountain.

Doubts and fears are the killers of faith. Many are fearful of what others might say, or how foolish they might look to someone important in their life. Others are afraid of failure or concerned that they might make a mistake.

---

[21] 2 Chronicles 20:1-30

[22] Deuteronomy 8:1-5

There are constant reminders of all of their past failures and shortcomings by voices seen and unseen. Sometimes doubts creep in and suggest that what God meant was mistaken, misread, misunderstood or worse. Some may even feel that they have somehow been misled. Ultimately if one is patient and persevering, the word spoken by the Lord will come to pass and one's faith will be rewarded.

In each aspect, God has clearly made His declarations. For Him they are established facts. They are available to those who accept them by faith, with nothing wavering. If one learns to operate by faith, then the response to every promise of God is "yes" and our response is "amen"[23] (so let it be).

The Covenants

In the Introduction the language of the old covenant was mentioned. This is also a key foundational aspect of understanding the gift of God in Christ. First of all, a covenant is an agreement between two parties. Those parties can be individuals, families, or even communities or nations. Specific promises are made between the two parties and as long as those promises are kept, the covenant remains in force. If not, then the covenant is broken, cancelled and considered null and void. There are many kinds of covenants, but one covenant that warrants our consideration is the blood covenant.

This New Covenant would be nothing like the Sinai Covenant

[23] 2 Corinthians 1:20

God's Covenant with Abraham

In a blood covenant the agreement was sealed with blood. In Genesis 15, God renewed a promise made earlier to Abram. God originally told Abram to leave his home and family, go to a land that He would show him, and He would make of Abram a great nation. Unfortunately, he and his wife Sarai had no children. Over the course of their conversation Abram asks for assurances to these promises. He says "how will I know that I will take possession of it?" (the land of his promised inheritance). God then asked Abram to do what might seem odd to us, but the patriarch understood clearly. Various animals were to be killed, split in half and the pieces arranged in a row with the halves opposite each other. The blood would drain toward each other creating a pathway of blood between the carcasses. After negotiating the parties in a blood covenant would come to an agreement. They would then walk in between these pieces in the bloody pathway and recite the terms of the covenant and the promises made to one another. In effect, they would be saying "may what happened to these animals happen to me if I do not do what I have promised today."

As the sun was setting, God both prophesied and confirmed the promises He made to Abram. A smoking firepot and a blazing torch appeared and passed between the pieces. In fact, the Great Sovereign God of the universe stooped to make a blood covenant to assure a man that He was willing to bind Himself to what He had promised, the way men of that day did.

Notice that God did not allow Abram to walk the split pieces of animals and birds with Him. He put him to sleep. A smoking fire pot and a torch passed between the pieces.

God, who is a consuming fire, covenanted with Himself on behalf of Abram.[24] Had Abram walked the pieces with God when he broke faith by sleeping with Hagar, he would have had to pay the penalty of breaking the covenant with his life.

Often when others listen to many Christians and those who purport to speak for Christianity, everything seems to hinge on the faithfulness of the believer, but in fact the real core of the believer's faith rests on God's faithfulness.[25] It is about God's willingness to stand by and back up His Word.

The Old Covenant

Four hundred thirty years later at Mount Sinai, God entered into another blood covenant. After reminding the Israelites that He brought them out of Egypt, God spoke in thunderous tones the terms of His covenant with them. They were written in stone with the finger of God. After the worship of a golden calf, Moses received a replacement set of the words of the covenant, the Ten Commandments, for the ones symbolically broken by Moses.[26]

Upon hearing the terms of the covenant, the people declared "Everything the Lord has said we will do." The people were all sprinkled with blood sealing and confirming the covenant. The basis for the Sinai Covenant was that human effort would be employed to follow the commands of the Lord in exchange for His blessing and favor. Any violation of the terms of the covenant brought dire consequences.

---

[24] See Isaiah 42:6. There the Servant of the Lord Himself is the covenant for the people. Again, we see God covenanting with Himself on behalf of those He wishes to bless.

[25] 2 Timothy 11-13

[26] See Exodus 19-24

The "do or die" language of the old covenant created a motivation of fear and fear of punishment. God was viewed as an exacting and vengeful tyrant eager to show what happens when one disobeyed. It also did not help that the Israelites were so prone to assimilate the idolatrous practices of the neighboring peoples and kingdoms. In spite of warning after warning, and prophet after prophet sent to bring the Israelites back to the remembrance of the covenant, by the time of Christ, God was ready to make a major change.

The New Covenant

The prophets Isaiah, Jeremiah and Ezekiel prophesied about the current conditions and the upcoming exile of the people of Israel and Judah. There also began to emerge predictions about a new covenant.

In Hebrews Chapter 8, the writer revealed through the Spirit that the change from the old to the new covenant was "better." Jesus was a better mediator and this covenant was "founded on better promises." For "if there had been nothing wrong with the first covenant, no place would have been sought for another."

The old covenant was based on the human efforts of the people of Israel to do all that they said that they would do. However, the new covenant was based on believing and receiving by faith the things that God promised that He would do in and for them.

The prophet Jeremiah introduces this New Covenant:

"The time is coming," declares the Lord,
"when I will make a new covenant
with the house of Israel
and with the house of Judah.
It will not be like the covenant
I made with their forefathers
when I took them by the hand
to lead them out of Egypt,
because they broke my covenant,
though I was a husband to them,"
declares the Lord.
"This is the covenant I will make with the house of Israel
after that time," declares the Lord.
"I will put my law in their minds
and write it on their hearts.
I will be their God,
and they will be my people.
No longer will a man teach his neighbor,
or a man his brother, saying, 'Know the Lord,'
because they will all know me,
from the least of them to the greatest,"
declares the Lord.
"For I will forgive their wickedness and will remember their sins no more."[27]

When the Lord introduced this New Covenant He specifically stated that it would be nothing like the Sinai Covenant. The Old Covenant, as stated earlier was based on strict adherence to its terms. A close and careful reading of the New Covenant reveals however that God repeatedly states what He will do without explicitly listing what the other party is to do. The implied requirement is to believe and receive what He is offering. The believer is asked to receive the benefits of this covenant by faith.

[27] Jeremiah 31:31-34

There are basically three terms of this covenant:

1. Although listed last, the first provision deals with the sin problem once and for all. God reveals that He would "forgive their wickedness and will remember their sins no more." Only by accomplishing this provision could He go on to provide the other two.

2. He would recreate and rewire their internal motivations by placing His "laws in their minds and write it on their hearts." The prophet Ezekiel further elaborates on this by predicting that God would give them "a new heart and put a new spirit in them" and "remove the stony heart and give [them] a heart of flesh."[28]

3. The last provision was that He would provide for direct communion with every believer. Under the Old Covenant only prophets could communicate directly with God and if they wanted to communicate with God they would have to seek one out, even if they were a king. However, under the New Covenant "they will all know Me from the least of them to the greatest."

There is a contrast throughout the New Testament between the old and the new covenant. John begins his gospel saying that the law came through Moses, but grace and truth came through Jesus Christ.[29] In Galatians the distinctions between the covenants is illustrated throughout the book by various contrasts: faith and observing the law; the law and the promise; slaves and sons; Hagar and Sarah; freedom in Christ and bondage; life in the Spirit and being

---

[28] See Ezekiel 36:24-27

[29] John 1:12

under the law. In 2 Corinthians 3:6-18 the contrast is as follows: the letter that kills and the Spirit that gives life; the ministry that brought death engraved in letters on stone that was connected to Moses, as opposed to the ministry of the Spirit; and the ministry that condemns verses the ministry that brings righteousness.

In the old covenant the temple was where God's presence was and only a select few, even among the priests, were privileged, on rare occasions, to enter into His presence. In the new covenant, the believer's body is the temple of the Holy Ghost and not only can His presence be with each one all the time, but everyone can enter boldly into the throne room of God through prayer at any time in Jesus' name. Every believer, then, is a priest who can approach and minister to God. As the writer of Hebrews said, it is based on better promises.

The core of the new covenant is faith in what God said He would do. What He did was to provide the solution for all of the problems in us that the old covenant pointed out, but could not fix. The first problem that God had to address was His own wrath and He offered this freely to us as a gift.

Chapter 3

THE GIFT OF PEACE

The soul who sins is the one who will die. The son will not share the guilt of the father, nor will the father share the guilt of the son. The righteousness of the righteous man will be credited to him, and the wickedness of the wicked will be charged against him (Ezekiel 18:20).

The wrath of God is being revealed from heaven against all the godlessness and wickedness of men who suppress the truth by their wickedness, since what may be known about God is plain to them, because God has made it plain to them (Romans 1:18-19).

And he is the propitiation for our sins: and not for ours only, but also for the sins of the whole world. Herein is love, not that we loved God, but that he loved us, and sent his Son to be the propitiation for our sins (1 John 2:2; 4:10 KJV).

When Christ came as high priest of the good things that are already here, he went through the greater and more perfect tabernacle that is not man-made, that is to say, not a part of this creation. He did not enter by means of the blood of goats and calves; but he entered the Most Holy Place once for all by his own blood, having obtained eternal redemption. The blood of goats and bulls and the ashes of a heifer sprinkled on those who are ceremonially unclean sanctify them so that they are outwardly clean. How much more, then, will the blood of Christ, who through the eternal Spirit offered himself unblemished to God, cleanse our consciences from acts that lead to death, so that we may serve the living God! (Hebrews 9:11-14).

As for you, you were dead in your transgressions and sins, in which you used to live when you followed the ways of this world and of the ruler of the kingdom of the air, the spirit who is now at work in those who are disobedient. All of us also lived among them at one time, gratifying the cravings of our sinful nature and following its desires and thoughts. Like the rest, we were by nature objects of wrath. But because of his great love for us, God, who is rich in mercy, made us alive with Christ even when we were dead in transgressions—it is by grace you have been saved. And God raised us up with Christ and seated us with him in the heavenly realms in Christ Jesus, in order that in the coming ages he might show the incomparable riches of his grace, expressed in his kindness to us in Christ Jesus. For it is by grace you have been saved, through faith—and this not from yourselves, it is the gift of God—not by works, so that no one can boast. For we are God's workmanship, created in Christ Jesus to do good works, which God prepared in advance for us to do.

Therefore, remember that formerly you who are Gentiles by birth and called "uncircumcised" by those who call themselves "the circumcision" (that done in the body by the hands of men)—remember that at that time you were separate from Christ, excluded from citizenship in Israel and foreigners to the covenants of the promise, without hope and without God in the world. But now in Christ

Jesus you who once were far away have been brought near through the blood of Christ.

For he himself is our peace, who has made the two one and has destroyed the barrier, the dividing wall of hostility, by abolishing in his flesh the law with its commandments and regulations. His purpose was to create in himself one new man out of the two, thus making peace, and in this one body to reconcile both of them to God through the cross, by which he put to death their hostility. He came and preached peace to you who were far away and peace to those who were near. For through him we both have access to the Father by one Spirit (Ephesians 2:1-18).

Under normal circumstances, if an ordinary cat encounters an equally ordinary dog, the reaction will be predictable. The cat will arch its back, start to hiss and prepare to fight. The dog would bare its teeth, growl and ready itself for battle. The reason for this is because cats and dogs are natural enemies. Neither animal need ever have seen each other before. Merely being in proximity of each other elicits the same antagonistic involuntary reaction.

God's reaction to the rebellion against His authority by Adam, called sin in the Bible, would be just as immediate as that of a dog when it sees a cat. However, it would be infinitely more intense and instantly deadly were it not for His mercy. It is only because of His mercy that we are not consumed.[1] Without that loving attribute in God's character, the moment the rebellion of sin was introduced into the earth, it and whatever was connected to it, would have been instantly obliterated, whether these things were plants, animals, people, houses and businesses. Anything connected to Adam, as the recognized head of the race established by God, would share his fate.

The only thing that would satisfy God's wrath is the death of a sinner

There are examples of this wrath against sin with Sodom and Gomorrah and in the wilderness among the Israelites. In the case of Sodom, God's mercy ran out. Through the prophet Ezekiel, God revealed why it was destroyed. The prophet lists unconcern and insensitivity to the poor and the needy, its pride and detestable and deplorable practices as the actions that invited His stern, yet righteous judgment and wrath.[2] After removing the nephew of His friend Abram, God

[1] Lamentations 3:22
[2] Ezekiel 16:49-50

rained fire and brimstone on the cities of the plain annihilating them forever.[3]

On the wilderness journey to Canaan, God's wrath was again shown as severe and, in this case, immediate. The word records murmuring dissent and complaining from some people dissatisfied with the hardships of the trip through the wilderness and God's chosen leaders. Day after day of the same food, scarce water and following a route to their destination that seemed to make no sense, tested their patience. Some failed the test. While the words of discontent and complaining were still in their mouths, fire shot out from the cloud that surrounded the presence of the Lord and consumed them instantly.[4]

Sin produces death. Left on its own it will eventually kill the one that indulges in it and is infected by it. It is like cancer or leprosy[5] that eats away at the organs or skin until it finally takes the life of its victim.

However, sin cannot exist in the presence of a holy and righteous God. When God sent an Angel to guard the way of the children of Israel on their way to Canaan, they were warned to be very careful not to rebel against what the angel said because he would not forgive their rebellion. The reason was because God's Name was in him,[6] meaning that His holy and righteous character was a part of the angel. In ancient times a person's name indicated what kind of person he was; it was an expression of his character. His actions would be exactly like God's with regard to rebellion and sin.

Sinners do what they do because they were born that way

The term used in the Bible to describe God's reaction and attitude towards sin and sinners is wrath. Sinners are

[3] Genesis 18:16-19:29

[4] Numbers 11:1-3

[5] See Isaiah 1:5-6

[6] Exodus 23:20-21

called objects of His wrath.[7] Even though it seems as if nothing happens to people who do wrong continually, God's wrath is still on them. It is stored up to be poured out at a certain point in time.[8]

It should be pointed out that a person is not a sinner because of an act that violates a law or commandment. Sinners do what they do (sin) because they were born that way. Men are identified as sinners because the law points out the actions of sinners. Man sins because he was born a sinner. It is in his nature. It is because of one man's sin (Adam) that all men and women became sinners.[9] As the head of the family of man, his choices have affected everyone and everything under his dominion.

Sinners are called objects of His wrath

When we were born, we had no choice about many things; our hair, skin and eye color, who our parents were, etc. In addition to that, we were born connected to and controlled by sin because of Adam's choice in the Garden of Eden. Everyone born since Adam is under the penalty of death. They are also the object of God's wrath.

Before the eating of the fruit of the tree of the knowledge of good and evil, Adam had direct and unveiled contact with God. However, since that time no son of Adam could even approach Him because of His holy and righteous nature. He would be instantly destroyed. Even holy prophets felt totally wretched and unclean in His presence.[10] Fear and terror gripped the children of Israel and even Moses.[11]

The only thing that would satisfy God's wrath is the death of the sinner. He said the soul that sins shall die.[12]

---

[7] Romans 1:18-19 and Ephesians 2:3
[8] Romans 2:5-11
[9] Romans 5:12
[10] See Isaiah 6:1-7
[11] Exodus 20:18-21 and Hebrews 12:18-21
[12] Ezekiel 18:4, 20

Sinners were dealt with quickly and severely throughout the Bible, especially in the Old Testament, but God in His mercy provided a way to satisfy His own wrath and to allow for sons of Adam to approach Him freely without fear.

The Propitiation

There are a few places in the Word of God where Jesus is called propitiation.[13] Propitiation is an offering that turns away God's wrath. It is similar to those old Greek stories of sea monsters or horrible beasts that would terrorize a coastal town or territory. The only thing that would save the town and appease the demigod was a virgin sacrifice. The townspeople would select some young woman who would be left at some agreed upon location to be devoured or taken by the beast. His wrath or anger assuaged, the god would spare the town or region; that is until he got mad again.[14] A closer look at Jesus' prayer in the garden of Gethsemane will help us understand this term propitiation.

When Jesus was in the garden of Gethsemane, He asked the Father "If it were possible to let this cup pass from me."[15] What was the "cup" that He was praying about? Was it the pressure of His approaching death, or the horrible manner of His death on the cross?

A death by execution on a Roman cross was an especially horrific way to die. The man was shamed in that he hanged on the cross naked. The wounds in his hands and feet were not life threatening but very painful. His body was configured in such a way that the weight of it slumped down, pulling on the wounds, causing excruciating pain and contracting his lungs so that the man could not breathe. The only way for a man to expand his lungs enough to inhale was to push up on

[13] 1 John 2:2; 4:10 (KJV)

[14] The films Clash of the Titans, (1981) MGM and (2010) Warner Brothers, both depict that scenario.

[15] Matthew 26:3; Mark 14:35 and Luke 22:41-44

the nails that secured his hands and feet to the cross and stretch his torso and expand his lungs enough to inhale a few quick breaths. The pain would be so severe that he could only maintain that position for just a few seconds at a time. This would go on for hours, days and weeks, depending on the strength, endurance and will power of the condemned man.[16]

Many men died bravely on the cross as depicted accurately in the film *Spartacus*.[17] To think that Jesus prayed so intensely about something that other ordinary men faced bravely is inconsistent with the resolute and courageous Man portrayed in the gospels.

That "cup" may very well have been what the Bible calls the wine of the wrath of God.[18] In Revelation there is the phrase, the cup of God's wrath or the wine of the wrath of God poured out without measure into the cup of His indignation.[19] It is the full extent of God's wrath without any mercy.

Remember, Jesus would not be taking on the wrath of God for just one sinner, but for every sinner. From Adam to the last child that will ever be born, Jesus took on God's full wrath in their place. Imagine the multiplied wrath of the sins of trillions of men who have lived on the earth poured out on one man!

Instead of putting His wrath on us the Father chose to direct it toward His Son who had no sin in (being born by the Holy Ghost through a virgin) or on Him because He was sinless. Legally, He had no reason to face that wrath.

Everyone who believes and receives the Gift of His Son is freed from God's wrath. Those who refuse by unbelief for whatever reason still have God's wrath on them.[20] Those

---

[16] For more information about a death on a Roman cross see The Day Christ Died by Jim Bishop, Harper Collins Publishing 1991

[17] (1960) Universal Pictures

[18] Isaiah 51:17-22

[19] Revelation 14:10

[20] John 3:36

who believe and receive Him are saved from God's wrath through Him.[21] In effect, God bore His own wrath for us.

The Peace Offering

One of the first sacrifices that an Israelite had to make at the temple was a peace offering. That offering required the blood of the sacrificed animal to be sprinkled on the altar and then it was burned on the altar. The man had to lay his hands on the head of the animal first. This sacrifice would create peace, or fellowship between the offerer and God.

Jesus Himself is our peace offering.[22] We are also reconciled to God.[23] This means that the one who puts his or her faith in Jesus, God's wrath has already been satisfied and there is peace or fellowship with God through Jesus' blood, giving the believer confidence of complete and unfettered access to God.

This peace is also a major part of the internal wiring and uniqueness of the believer. In the midst of trying circumstances, perplexing problems and dire straits there is, or will be, a supernatural peace. These attacks, in fact, are tests sent to challenge the believer's confidence in the word from God. Jesus predicted trouble and tribulation in the experience of those who would follow Him, but promised them peace. It would not be an ordinary peace or one that the world gives that is dependent on serene circumstances. He called it "My peace."[24] A peace that is not affected by anything that the world can throw at it. It is also called "the peace of God"[25] that acts like a sentry that guards

In effect, God bore His own wrath for us

[21] Romans 5:9
[22] Ephesians 2:14
[23] 2 Corinthians 5:18-19 and Ephesians 2:14-18
[24] John 14:27
[25] Philippians 4:4-8

the trusting believer's heart and mind from distress, despair and crippling depression. The wicked know no peace,[26] but the Lord of peace, as Paul calls Him, verifies His presence in the lives of His followers with peace in the midst of intense and violent storms.[27] While others panic he has a peace that surpasses all understanding.[28]

Finally, the only reason believers can pray and commune with God is because His wrath and anger was placed on Jesus. We receive God's fellowship or friendship through Jesus with whom God says He is well pleased.

Unfortunately, many look at the things that they do: good works, going to church and such things that please God. In actuality, however, only His Son pleases Him. By accepting God's wrath on our behalf, Jesus also pleased the Father by created access to Him for us. The Father loved sinners so much that He wanted to have fellowship with them. Jesus provided that solution in His own body. His willingness to offer Himself as the solution also pleased the Father. By faith in Jesus, the gift of God, His wrath is appeased; we have peace with Him, access to Him and fellowship with Him.

[26] Isaiah 48:22
[27] See Mark 4:35-41
[28] Philippians 4:7

Chapter 4

The Gift of Death

For Christ's love compels us, because we are convinced that one died for all, and therefore all died. And he died for all, that those who live should no longer live for themselves but for him who died for them and was raised again (2 Corinthians 5:14-15).

Or don't you know that all of us who were baptized into Christ Jesus were baptized into his death? We were therefore buried with him through baptism into death in order that, just as Christ was raised from the dead through the glory of the Father, we too may live a new life. If we have been united with him like this in his death, we will certainly also be united with him in his resurrection. For we know that our old self was crucified with him so that the body of sin might be done away with, that we should no longer be slaves to sin—because anyone who has died has been freed from sin. Now if we died with Christ, we believe that we will also live with him. For we know that since Christ was raised from the dead, he cannot die again; death no longer has mastery over him. The death he died, he died to sin once for all; but the life he lives, he lives to God. In the same way, count yourselves dead to sin but alive to God in Christ Jesus (Romans 6:3-11).

Since you died with Christ to the basic principles of this world, why, as though you still belonged to it, do you submit to its rules: "Do not handle! Do not taste! Do not touch!" These are all destined to perish with use, because they are based on human commands and teachings. Such regulations indeed have an appearance of wisdom, with their self-imposed worship, their false humility and their harsh treatment of the body, but they lack any value in restraining sensual indulgence (Colossians 2:20-23).

Here is a trustworthy saying: If we died with him, we will also live with him; if we endure, we will also reign with him. If we disown him, he will also disown us; if we are faithless, he will remain faithful, for he cannot disown himself (2 Timothy 2:11-13).

For through the law I died to the law so that I might live for God. I have been crucified with Christ and I no longer live, but Christ lives in me. The life I live in the body, I live by faith in the Son of God, who loved me and gave himself for me. I do not set aside the grace of God, for if righteousness could be gained through the law, Christ died for nothing!" (Galatians 2:19-21).

Do you not know, brothers—for I am speaking to men who know the law—that the law has authority over a man only as long as he lives? For example, by law a married woman is bound to her husband as long as he is alive, but if her husband dies, she is released from the law of marriage. So then, if she marries another man while her husband is still alive, she is called an adulteress. But if her husband dies, she is released from that law and is not an adulteress, even though she marries another man. So, my brothers, you also died to the law through the body of Christ, that you might belong to another, to him who was raised from the dead, in order that we might bear fruit to God. For when we were controlled by the sinful nature, the sinful passions aroused by the law were at work in our bodies, so that we bore fruit for death. But now, by dying to what once bound us, we have been released from the law so that we serve in the new way of the Spirit, and not in the old way of the written code (Romans 7:1-6).

What then shall we say? That the Gentiles, who did not pursue righteousness, have obtained it, a righteousness that is by faith; but Israel, who pursued a law of righteousness, has not attained it. Why not? Because they pursued it not by faith but as if it were by works. They stumbled over the "stumbling stone." As it is written: "See, I lay in Zion a stone that causes men to stumble and a rock that makes them fall, and the one who trusts in him will never be put to shame." Brothers, my heart's desire and prayer to God for the Israelites is that they may be saved. For I can testify about them that they are zealous for God, but their zeal is not based on knowledge. Since they did not know the righteousness that comes from God and sought to establish their own, they did not submit to God's righteousness. Christ is the end of the law so that there may be righteousness for everyone who believes (Romans 9:30-10:4).

You foolish Galatians! Who has bewitched you? Before your very eyes Jesus Christ was clearly portrayed as crucified. I would like to learn just one thing from you: Did you receive the Spirit by observing the law, or by believing what you heard? Are you so foolish? After beginning with the Spirit, are you now trying to attain your goal by human effort? Have you suffered so much for nothing—if it really was for nothing? Does God give you his Spirit and work miracles among you because you observe the law, or because you believe what you heard? Consider Abraham: "He believed God, and it was credited to him as righteousness." Understand, then, that those who believe are children of Abraham. The Scripture foresaw that God would justify the Gentiles by faith, and announced the gospel in advance to Abraham: "All nations will be blessed through you." So those who have faith are blessed along with Abraham, the man of faith. All who rely on observing the law are under a curse, for it is written: "Cursed is everyone who does not continue to do everything written in the Book of the Law." Clearly no one is justified before God by the law, because, "The righteous will live by faith." The law is not based on faith; on the contrary, "The man who does these things will live by them." Christ redeemed us from the curse of the law by becoming a curse for us, for it is written: "Cursed is everyone who is hung on a tree." He redeemed us in order that the blessing given to Abraham might come to the Gentiles through Christ Jesus, so that by faith we might receive the promise of the Spirit (Galatians 3:1-14).

In the last chapter, the death of the sinner was established as the only thing that would satisfy God's wrath. The Lord Jesus accepted the full wrath of God on behalf of all men thereby making peace and reconciliation between God and man possible.

The law exposes everyone's flaws, shortcomings, selfishness and flesh

Death, however, is also one of the gifts received from God through Jesus. By His death individual sins are remitted, the condemnation and jurisdiction of the law was removed, the flesh (sinful nature) was dealt with and the last will and testament has been read. The benefits of which will be discussed in the next two chapters.

The Sin Offering

The sanctuary system of the old covenant was a teaching tool to give a glimpse of what was to come in the body of Christ. The various sacrifices and ceremonies all pointed in one way or another to some aspect of what we receive through Jesus.

One such example is the sin offering. This offering was very specific. If someone committed a sin, a spotless lamb without any blemishes would be brought to the temple. The sin was transferred to the lamb by laying one's hands on its head and the specific transgression was confessed. The throat of the lamb was cut severing the artery in the unsuspecting animal's neck. Then, as the blood spewed out with every beat of the quivering creature's heart, it was collected and sprinkled on the altar and the body, or most of it, was burned there as well.[1] Every sin required a separate sacrifice. So with hundreds of thousands coming

---

[1] Leviticus 4:1-5:13

annually to the Temple there was a huge number of sin sacrifices made daily. Imagine if that had to be done today for every single act of transgression.

One of the main messages of this ceremony was to instruct, in as graphic a way as possible, the cost of every act of transgression. Death was required, but more than just simple death; death by the shedding of blood.

The Israelites were forbidden to eat meat with the blood still in it.[2] God said that it was given to make atonement for one's life because the life was in the blood.[3] In Hebrews, the writer states that without the shedding of blood there is no remission[4] (or payment and cancellation of the debt) of sins. Remember, for each act of sin and each transgression, blood must be shed. It must be shed in such a way that results in the death of the sacrifice.

Your confidence is now in God's Word, not your ability to perform

It is not the blood of bulls and goats but the precious blood of Jesus that cleanses the believer from and remits or pays for all of his sins. This was done one time, for everyone, for every single sin that has been or will ever be committed. That means before anyone alive today was born, the blood was shed to atone for every single act of transgression for every human being. This provision has been available for every individual that has lived or will ever live on the earth. This, however, is available only by faith. If one does not believe and receive Him by faith, nothing that is offered freely will be realized. It is not automatic.

In the book of the Psalms David wrote about the one who receives this aspect of the grace offered by God. He writes that "Blessed is he whose transgressions are

[2] Leviticus 17
[3] Leviticus 17:11
[4] Hebrews 9:22

forgiven, whose sins are covered. Blessed is the man whose sin the Lord does not count against him in whose spirit there is no deceit."[5]

In the last phrase of that passage the Psalmist writes that God does not count this blessed man's sins against him. In Romans 4:15 Paul explains this to mean that the Father keeps no list or record for those who operate by faith in His Son.[6]

Bear in mind that the problem of sin created a major dilemma for God. As a loving Father, He wanted to forgive and show mercy. Yet, as a righteous Judge, He could not simply let the guilty go free. His solution was to place the penalty of death for every act of transgression ever committed upon His Son.

Since the penalty for each sin has already been paid, the believer will not have his sin counted against him. Each and every act of rebellion that has ever been or will ever be committed, no matter how disgusting or despicable, has been paid for in full by the Blood of Jesus. God did this to demonstrate His justice and yet still be the One who justifies (declares as righteous) those who have faith in His Son.[7]

Christ is the end, destination and goal of the law

A Definition of Transgression

One of the ways we know what sin is by the instrument God introduced to point it out: the Ten Commandment Law. One definition of sin states that sin is the transgression of the law.[8] It is called a schoolmaster.[9] It is also called a

[5] Psalm 32:1-2
[6] See 2 Corinthians 5:17-19
[7] Romans 3:26
[8] 1 John 1:9 (KJV)
[9] Galatians 3:24 (KJV)

mirror[10] that one looks at to determine, for instance, if their face needs washing. It is holy, just and good,[11] but its only function is to point out and identify sin.

It is similar to that special chemical that causes blood to display a special glow under certain lights that crime scene investigators use called Luminal. Even if a criminal uses soap and water, under a special light, even the smallest traces of blood will show up if this chemical is sprayed on it. The bathroom may look spotless, but that light can expose evidence of a hideous crime scene.

So, the law exposes everyone's flaws, shortcomings, selfishness and flesh. It also condemns men as sinners. It points the accusing finger at us, identifying everyone as transgressors and also reminds sinners that anyone who sins must die.

The law condemns, accuses, curses and sentences to death

The law condemns, accuses, curses and sentences to death. Its ministry engraved in letters on stone, brought death. It provides nothing to remedy the problem of sin; it only points it out. Whether one is aware of it or not, everyone is under its condemnation and jurisdiction. Just as an over-anxious policeman, the law is ready to both cite and punish even the smallest (so to speak) infraction. And the penalty is always the same, death.

Many use strict obedience to the law as the means to attain favor from God and righteousness like the Israelites did. Unfortunately, the Israelites could never attain it and neither will those who continue to try to do that now. The reason, as will be discussed later, is the sinful nature of man, commonly known as the flesh in the Bible.

---

[10] James 1:22-25, 2:8-11

[11] Romans 7:12

The Flesh

There is also what Paul calls "the law of sin" or the flesh. Everyone is born with a nature that is controlled by the selfish desires of sin. It does not have to be learned, it is inbred. The desires of lust, pride, envy, greed, avarice, strife, hate and every other sinful tendency is in us at birth. This, we inherited from our forefather, Adam, as well as sickness and death among other things that will be elaborated on later. Some traits are stronger in some than others, but it all comes from the same source, our sinful flesh.

What many may not realize is that the flesh has a positive side. Even though it is positive, it is still sinful flesh.[12] Paul describes it in Philippians. Normally, flesh is described as the characteristics of the aforementioned list. However, Paul ascribes his covenant relationship to Abraham (circumcision), being part of the chosen people of an elite tribe (Benjamin, the tribe of Israel's first king), his strict adherence to the law (Pharisee), his willingness to put his beliefs into action (zeal), and his blameless behavior (legalistic righteousness) as flesh. The same kind of flesh as adultery, lust, greed and the like.[13]

... those who rely on their human effort to become righteous are actually under a curse

In other words, even doing good things out of human efforts is unacceptable because the source is tainted and corrupt. There are many Christians, churches and ministries, while well intended, inadvertently appeal to the flesh. Defining the problem, exposing sin and the enemy dominates many messages, rarely with a Biblical

---

[12] It should be noted that Watchman Nee's writings on the flesh strongly influenced this section. For more see his work entitled The Spiritual Man, Living Stream Ministry 1998.

[13] Philippians 3:2-6

solution other than, "try harder" or "do better." Ultimately all of our righteousness, however, is as filthy rags.[14]

The word, the Spirit and the law will always expose the defects, shortcomings and sin in one's life, but God's gift is not about the problem. He is the solution. When an understanding of The Father's Gift is absent, many employ human effort (flesh) to solve their problems. This, unfortunately, can often lead to frustration, never-ending guilt and hypocrisy. As a result many just simply give up.

Paul wrote that those who rely on their human effort to keep the law as a way to become righteous are actually under a curse.[15] He goes on to state that no one is justified (declared righteous) by the law.[16] Even holding on to the old covenant (the law) puts a veil or blinders on one's face.[17]

It is not that the law is evil: we are. It is holy and it is doing what it was designed to do. The law is misused and becomes counterproductive when it is combined with the inherent flesh and human efforts as a way to become righteous.

Jesus said, "Come to me all of you who labor and are heavy laden and I will give you rest."[18] That rest is from the hard work of trying to accomplish in the flesh what God offers freely through faith in His Son. Those who acknowledge the poverty of their spirit are the ones who inherit the kingdom of heaven. Those who mourn over their sinfulness will be comforted. Those who hunger and thirst for righteousness will be filled with the righteousness that comes by faith in Christ. Their righteousness will exceed the righteousness of the pharisees because it is a righteousness that comes from God Himself,[19] which is the only kind that He accepts.

---

[14] Isaiah 54:6
[15] Galatians 3:10-14
[16] Romans 3:19, 26 and Galatians 3:11
[17] 2 Corinthians 3:13-18
[18] Matthew 11:28 (KJV)
[19] Romans 3:22

In Romans 7, Paul described God's solution for the flesh and the condemning and unyielding jurisdiction of the law. He related a parable of the dilemma of a married woman to a very law-conscious audience. She no longer wanted to be married to her overbearing husband, but if she left him for another more acceptable mate she would be an adulterer. So what is the only solution? Death. If the mean husband dies, she is released to marry the other man.

The point of the illustration was not marriage and divorce, but God's solution for the law. All men were born sinners and the law demanded that the sentence be carried out. Everyone was condemned to death. So God saw to it that the sentence was carried out by His Son on behalf of the whole world. When Jesus died, for those who put their faith in Him, they also died. For those who put their trust in themselves or never put their trust in Jesus, the condemnation of the law will eventually be carried out on them.

Many may not realize that the flesh has a positive side

The believer has been crucified with Christ, by faith, yet he is still alive. The law demanded death, and God saw to it that the righteous demands of the law were met. There is now, therefore no condemnation from the law for anyone who has their faith in Christ Jesus.[20] By His blood all transgressions or individual acts of sin have been atoned for and, by his death, the law's demand for the death of the sinner has been satisfied.

Double Jeopardy

When Tim McVeigh, the accused, convicted and executed bomber of the Oklahoma City federal building, was still alive, there was a hearing about what would happen to parts of his body after his death. The judge ruled that anything that happened after Mr. McVeigh was dead was beyond his jurisdiction.

So it is with the law. Since we who believe died with Christ, the sentence of death has already been carried out. Therefore, we are beyond the jurisdiction of the law.

The legal term for this is "double jeopardy." It means that criminals cannot be tried, convicted (or acquitted) and sentenced twice for the same crime. By including the believer's death with Christ, the sentence of death was carried out and the offender is now free from the law's demands.

It is as if a convicted murderer had walked into the death chamber, the sentence was carried out and the doctor pronounced the prisoner dead. Suddenly, a few minutes later, should the man have gotten up, could the state execute him again? No. The sentence was carried out and he was confirmed dead by the state's physician. His debt to society has been paid. He would be free to go. He would no longer be under the condemnation of the law since the sentence had already been carried out.

This death did not only pay for a few sins. It paid for all of the believer's sins. Remember, the penalty was paid over 2000 years ago. This is thousands of years before we were born, yet all of those individual transgressions were placed on Jesus before they were actually committed. That, again, is why God does not count the believer's sins against him.

Jurisdiction Taken Away

Not only did our death with Christ take away the law's condemnation, but it also took away its jurisdiction or control over the believer. It is no longer a schoolmaster teaching and governing its pupils. Christ is the end, destination and goal of the law. All other substitutes, tutors, representatives, types or symbols become unnecessary and redundant. The guide in the believer's life is no longer a list of do's and don't's, but the Spirit of God now operates as the arbitrator of what to do and what not to do; what to say and what not to say; what to think and what not to think.

Guilt Eliminated

All of the guilt associated with sin and the condemnation of the law was also eliminated by the believer's death with Christ by faith. He carried all of our guilt and sorrow associated with sin.[20] He did that at the Father's request so that we can live a more abundant life and in complete freedom.

What all of this means is that by His blood, all of our actions, thoughts, and oversights called sins or transgressions have been paid for. The demand of the law for sinners to die has been satisfied. We are free from the jurisdiction of the law, again by dying with Jesus. All of this is by faith.

In Romans 6, Paul urges believers to "count yourselves dead." The word "count" in the KJV is translated "reckon." This word means to accept it as a fact. It is more than trying to sell yourself on the concept. It is believing it and receiving it. It is confessing it and walking in it. Paul, through The Holy Spirit, declared it, therefore it is so.

---

[20] See Isaiah 53:4-6 (KJV)

The Death of the Flesh

This counting one's self as dead also deals with the flesh. That sinful nature that we were born with through Adam is with us as long as we live. However, by dying, the flesh also died. Once that believer puts their faith in the free gift of the Father of His Son, His death also includes the death of their flesh or sinful nature. All of the tendencies, weaknesses, shortcomings, etc., that, as part of the flesh, also died with Him.

Remember, this is all by faith. A person may not feel different or look different. This is where many fail. They look for a change and when they do not sense any change, they assume that they did not receive anything.

Faith is not sight. We believe therefore, we speak it,[21] whether we see it, feel it or not. We, like our Father, speak things that are not as though they are.[22] God declared it; therefore it is whatever He said it is.

Even if the flesh tries to rise up through the subtle suggestions of the enemy, remind yourself and God in prayer making the confession that He declared you dead with Christ, so you expect His word to be more true than what you see and feel. Seeing is not believing. Believing first without evidence or proof will produce the manifestation of the thing promised. Wait on it. In God's timing it will appear.

---

[21] 2 Corinthians 4:13

[22] Romans 4:17b

The Symbolism of Baptism

The symbol of dying with Christ given to the apostles to pass on to the believer who put their faith in Christ was baptism. The actual act of baptism involves fully immersing an individual under water and bringing him or her up again. It is done this way because the word used in the Bible means to dip or immerse. The imagery is that of a fabric submerged into a solution of dye changing its color completely.

What is being symbolized is being buried and rising up again. By faith in Christ the believer has accepted the fact that he died with Jesus. He is symbolically buried with Him and has risen with Him. More will be discussed in the next chapter.

In effect, this is a public statement of faith in God. The believer is not making a promise to do good or change his or her life, as many believe. He is believing what God has said. The Father has already stated what He has done and what He will do for those who put their faith in His Son. The believer is declaring his belief in what God had freely given and trusting that anyone who puts his trust in Him will never be put to shame.[23] Again, seeing is not believing. In this walk, if we don't believe, we will never see. Our confidence is now in God's word, not our ability to perform.

The gift of death provided forgiveness for individual acts of transgressions through His blood. Through His death the believer is given freedom from the condemnation and jurisdiction of the law and the annihilation of the flesh. Then, God did something even greater. He provided for our death so that we can be born again.

[23] Romans 9:33b

Chapter 5

THE GIFT OF REBIRTH

In reply Jesus declared, "I tell you the truth, no one can see the kingdom of God unless he is born again." "How can a man be born when he is old?" Nicodemus asked. "Surely he cannot enter a second time into his mother's womb to be born!" Jesus answered, "I tell you the truth, no one can enter the kingdom of God unless he is born of water and the Spirit. Flesh gives birth to flesh, but the Spirit gives birth to spirit. You should not be surprised at my saying, 'You must be born again.' The wind blows wherever it pleases. You hear its sound, but you cannot tell where it comes from or where it is going. So it is with everyone born of the Spirit" (John 3:3-8).

And he died for all, that those who live should no longer live for themselves but for him who died for them and was raised again. So from now on we regard no one from a worldly point of view. Though we once regarded Christ in this way, we do so no longer. Therefore, if anyone is in Christ, he is a new creation; the old has gone, the new has come! All this is from God, who reconciled us to himself through Christ and gave us the ministry of reconciliation: that God was reconciling the world to himself in Christ, not counting men's sins against them. And he has committed to us the message of reconciliation. We are therefore Christ's ambassadors, as though God were making his appeal through us. We implore you on Christ's behalf: Be reconciled to God. God made him who had no sin to be sin for us, so that in him we might become the righteousness of God (2 Corinthians 5:15-21).

"If you love me, you will obey what I command. And I will ask the Father, and he will give you another Counselor to be with you forever—the Spirit of truth. The world cannot accept him, because it neither sees him nor knows him. But you know him, for he lives with you and will be in you. I will not leave you as orphans; I will come to you. Before long, the world will not see me anymore, but you will see me. Because I live, you also will live (John 14:15-19).

"All this I have spoken while still with you. But the Counselor, the Holy Spirit, whom the Father will send in my name, will teach you all things and will remind you of everything I have said to you (John 14:25-26).

"Now I am going to him who sent me, yet none of you asks me, 'Where are you going?' Because I have said these things, you are filled with grief. But I tell you the truth: It is for your good that I am going away. Unless I go away, the Counselor will not come to you; but if I go, I will send him to you. When he comes, he will convict the world of guilt in regard to sin and righteousness and judgment: in regard to sin, because men do not believe in me; in regard to righteousness, because I am going to the Father, where you can see me no longer; and in regard to judgment, because the prince of this world now stands condemned. "I have much more to say to you, more than you can now bear. But when he, the Spirit of truth, comes, he will guide you into all truth. He will not speak on his own; he will speak only what he hears, and he will tell you what is yet

to come. He will bring glory to me by taking from what is mine and making it known to you. All that belongs to the Father is mine. That is why I said the Spirit will take from what is mine and make it known to you (John 16:5-15).

In him we were also chosen, having been predestined according to the plan of him who works out everything in conformity with the purpose of his will, in order that we, who were the first to hope in Christ, might be for the praise of his glory. And you also were included in Christ when you heard the word of truth, the gospel of your salvation. Having believed, you were marked in him with a seal, the promised Holy Spirit, who is a deposit guaranteeing our inheritance until the redemption of those who are God's possession—to the praise of his glory (Ephesians 1:11-14).

Now it is God who makes both us and you stand firm in Christ. He anointed us, set his seal of ownership on us, and put his Spirit in our hearts as a deposit, guaranteeing what is to come (2 Corinthians 1:21-22).

So, my brothers, you also died to the law through the body of Christ, that you might belong to another, to him who was raised from the dead, in order that we might bear fruit to God. For when we were controlled by the sinful nature, the sinful passions aroused by the law were at work in our bodies, so that we bore fruit for death. But now, by dying to what once bound us, we have been released from the law so that we serve in the new way of the Spirit, and not in the old way of the written code (Romans 7:4-6).

Therefore, there is now no condemnation for those who are in Christ Jesus, because through Christ Jesus the law of the Spirit of life set me free from the law of sin and death. For what the law was powerless to do in that it was weakened by the sinful nature, God did by sending his own Son in the likeness of sinful man to be a sin offering. And so he condemned sin in sinful man, in order that the righteous requirements of the law might be fully met in us, who do not live according to the sinful nature but according to the Spirit. Those who live according to the sinful nature have their minds set on what that nature desires; but those who live in accordance with the Spirit have their minds set on what the Spirit desires. The mind of sinful man is death, but the mind controlled by the Spirit is life and peace; the sinful mind is hostile to God. It does not submit to God's law, nor can it do so. Those controlled by the sinful nature cannot please God. You, however, are controlled not by the sinful nature but by the Spirit, if the Spirit of God lives in you. And if anyone does not have the Spirit of Christ, he does not belong to Christ. But if Christ is in you, your body is dead because of sin, yet your spirit is alive because of righteousness. And if the Spirit of him who raised Jesus from the dead is living in you, he who raised Christ from the dead will also give life to your mortal bodies through his Spirit, who lives in you (Romans 8:1-11).

It was late at night. Most of the inhabitants of the city were asleep. A well-known leader of the religious council was quietly seeking Jesus to get some answers. Perhaps he had participated in discussions about this young prophet and teacher observing and admiring Him from a distance. He secretly approached Him at night to get a closer look at him away from the notice of others in the Sanhedrin. Little did Nicodemus realize that the answers to his many thoughtful, theological questions addressed the need of his heart and innermost being.

This is righteousness from God apart from the Law (see Romans 3:21), which is the only righteousness that He accepts.

He began by attempting to flatter Jesus, telling Him, "We know that you are a man sent from God." Jesus sidestepped the small talk and preliminaries and got right to the point. "You must be born again," He said to the strict commandment-keeping believer of Jehovah. Jesus went on to define what it means to be born again. Being born again comprised being born (or baptized) of the water and of the Spirit. Without being baptized both by the water and the Spirit, one is neither born again, nor will he even see, perceive, or comprehend the kingdom of God.

It is an exchange of one life for another, not simply an improvement of the former one

The last chapter introduced the baptism of the water. It is the acknowledgment of one's death: Death to the flesh, the condemnation and jurisdiction of the law and, by the Blood of Jesus, the payment for all individual acts of sin. Going down in the water, that is, being fully immersed under the water, symbolized being buried. However, the believer does not stay buried. He is brought up out of the water.

He has been raised to receive another aspect of God's gift: A new life led by and empowered by the Spirit of God. He, like everything else received from the Father through Jesus, is a free gift and not received because of one's goodness or effort. He is received by faith. God declared it, one believes and receives it without necessarily seeing any evidence and, according to the word, he shall have it.[1]

Throughout the scriptures there is an emphasis on God's requirement for righteousness in His people. For those who trusted in their own efforts under the old covenant, they declare like those at Mount Sinai, "Everything the Lord has said we will do."[2] Then, like those at the mount, they succeed for a while only to ultimately fail because of the flesh.

Communing is a two-way communication

God, however, had another way for a person to obtain righteousness; by His declaration. In Romans 4:3, Paul quoted Genesis 15:6 where the Spirit through Moses said "Abraham believed God and it was credited to him for righteousness." This righteousness was not something that came from Abraham. Abraham accepted the statement that God made about the innumerable descendants he would receive as a fact and, as a result of his faith, God declared Abraham righteous.

In the same way, by faith in Christ, God declares the ungodly righteous.[3] This is righteousness from God; His own righteousness freely given to the man or woman He chooses, which is the only righteousness that He accepts.[4] Therefore one can say as a result of their faith in Christ that they are righteous simply because God said so. He is the righteous Judge in these matters. His verdict is the only one that counts. And what He says is so, period.

---

1 See Mark 11:24
2 Exodus 24:3
3 Romans 5:4
4 Romans 3:21-22a

The Life of the Spirit

Baptism, as mentioned earlier, is the visible symbol of the believer's death with Christ. The sentence of death demanded by the law has been carried out. Every act of sin has been atoned or paid for by the Blood of Jesus. There is no condemnation of the law and it has no jurisdiction over the believer. This burial also is the death to everything inherited from Adam including the flesh or sinful nature. The believer, however, does not stay in the water. He rises to walk in a new life: the life of the Spirit.

In Galatians Paul described it this way, "I have been crucified with Christ, and I no longer live, but Christ lives in me."[5] He said in Romans that if we were united with Him in His death, we will certainly be united with Him in His resurrection. We were buried with Him in baptism and were raised to enter into a new life.[6] We were buried, then born again by His Spirit.

When Jesus died, He was placed in a tomb late on a Friday afternoon. Before daybreak on Sunday morning, by a power beyond anything that man can conceive or create, life came back into that body. We, like Jesus, died and were buried by faith. We then, based on God's Word, were raised by the same power that raised Christ Jesus into an entirely new life. Not a correction or a renovation of the old life because that has been buried. This is an entirely new, different and unique life.

The motivation to obey God and His Spirit is not based on fear

The language of the word is that Christ now lives by the Spirit of God within the believer.[7] In effect, it is an exchange of one life for another, not simply an improvement of the former one.

---

[5] Galatians 2:20

[6] Romans 6:1-7

[7] Romans 8:9-11

One of the dominant words in the religious world is change. One wants to change his or her life or change some habit or practice. Unfortunately, there are two problems with that approach:

1. One has no power to change and
2. God's solution was not to change or improve the person, but to facilitate his or her death through Jesus and place the life of the Son, who pleases Him, inside of the one who puts his or her complete faith and trust in His word.

God does not attempt to fix the old tree to produce good fruit.[8] He makes the tree all over completely from scratch. Any tree that does not produce good fruit is destroyed. By faith, the believer can choose which death he will experience. Either by participating in the death of Christ by faith, or personally in the punishment of fire prepared for the Devil and his angels.[9]

Those who by faith in Christ have died and were baptized into Christ, have also been clothed with Christ.[10] That person is an entirely new creation. Like God created the world from nothing, He recreates the believer from nothing. Everything that was connected to flesh, Adam and the law, including condemnation and its jurisdiction, is over; dead and gone. The Father makes those who believe alive with Christ. He raised Jesus from the dead and He will also give life to our mortal bodies through His Spirit who lives in us,[11] because the Spirit gives life and the flesh (human effort and anything related to it and the first Adam) counts for nothing.[12]

Everything hinges on His faithfulness. That is what counts

[8] Matthew 7:15-20, 12:33
[9] Matthew 25:41
[10] Romans 13:14 and Galatians 3:27
[11] Romans 8:9-11
[12] John 6:63

Remember, faith has to grab hold of what God says is there, even if there is no evidence in our feelings or senses that it exists. The Spirit of God through Paul stated that if one is baptized into Christ they has been clothed with Him. Confess it. Speak it. Remind yourself and the Father of it often in prayer, and it will come to pass according to His word.

In John 6, Jesus' disciples asked what kind of work did the Father require. Jesus answered that the work that God required was to believe in the One He has sent. It sounds easier than it really is. To believe in Christ and the fullness of what is offered freely in Him often goes against logic, so called common sense, the flesh (both positive and negative flesh), traditional church teachings, and opposition from friends and family. It sounds to the religious, like nonsense and to the worldly, like foolishness.[13]

In the parable of the sower, Jesus described how many who would hear and would receive the seed of the word about His kingdom. One group hears but does not understand. The enemy, like a bird eating the seed on the ground, snatches the word away before it can take root. He will also attack either by the pressures of life that will try to choke it out or with a myriad of other deceitful means. The next two groups receive the word with joy. However, when trouble, difficulties or persecution comes because of the word, they fall away. For others, the pursuit of wealth, which Jesus said is deceitful, chokes the life out of the seed. The last group receives and understands the word, allows it to take root then, eventually bears fruit.[14]

God, however, gives life to the dead and calls things that are not as though they are.[15] What He says is what counts. Everything we see came into existence with a word from His mouth: every plant, tree, grasshopper, butterfly, bird, hill, mountain, planet, star, solar system or galaxy. He

[13] See 1 Corinthians 1:22-25

[14] See the Parable of the Sower in Matthew 13:3-8, 18-23; Mark 4:3-8, 14-20 and Luke 8:5-8, 11-15

[15] Romans 4:17

will watch His Word to see to it that it accomplishes what He sent it to do.[16] Believe and trust in that more than what is seen, and it will be so.

More Definitions for Sin

Earlier there was a biblical definition for sin mentioned, but there are two other definitions found in the gospel of John and Romans. In John 16:9, Jesus says that the Holy Ghost would convict men of sin "because men do not believe in me." Many call on His name, but they place their faith and trust in other things: money, demonstrations, religious traditions, pastors, science, what everybody says, common wisdom or government. Often this is out of ignorance because many simply do not understand what is offered through Christ or how to receive it.

The other definition is in Romans and it simply states that everything that does not come from faith is sin.[17] Faith is the only thing that pleases the Father.[18] That faith comes by hearing the Word of God,[19] and the Word or the scriptures, according to Jesus, testifies of Him.[20] The believer's most strenuous effort will be to believe, trust and hold on to the word spoken and revealed by His Spirit in the face of contrary circumstances, evidence and pressures. Once again, as recorded in 2 Corinthians, one must believe and therefore speak.[21] The prophet Joel writes, "Let the weak say I'm strong."[22] God has promised, therefore believe it, confess it and walk in it.

The goal of the New Covenant is to produce sons of God

[16] Isaiah 55:11
[17] Romans 14:32b
[18] Hebrews 11:6
[19] Romans 10:17 (KJV)
[20] John 5:38-39
[21] 2 Corinthians 4:13
[22] Joel 3:10b

The Promise of the Father

The last chapter explored the illustration of a married woman in Romans 7. Her dilemma was solved by the death of one husband so that she was free to marry another. Paul concludes his example by reminding the readers that since we died with Christ, we are released from the condemnation and jurisdiction of the law to serve in the new way of the Spirit.

The promise of the Father, the outpouring of the Holy Spirit, was a significant emphasis of the apostles. First, the Spirit would quicken each believer to live a life motivated by a new nature. Then He would be a Guide that walks beside them. Finally, He would give each an empowerment to be effective witnesses for Christ. After receiving Him, the Spirit would lead them into all truth, live in them and tell them what to say when called upon to witness for Christ. He was called the "Paraclete." A paraclete is a Greek word that means "one who walks beside." The Spirit, then, is a guide, a teacher and a counselor. Rather than being led by rules, regulations, do's and don't's, these born again believers are led and guided by the Spirit.

Discerning and Hearing God's Voice

The first step in this walk of the Spirit is to hear and recognize the voice of the Spirit. Jesus said my sheep know my voice and a stranger's voice they will not listen to and run away.[23] In Isaiah 31:21, the Spirit says that you will hear a voice behind you saying this is the way, walk in it. This is dramatically illustrated in the early life of the prophet Samuel. When he was just a boy, God called him by name, but because he did not yet know the Lord, he did not recognize God's voice. After three attempts, he was still confusing

[23] John 10:1-18

God's voice with that of his elderly mentor, the High Priest Eli. After consulting with Eli, Samuel finally responded to the voice of God.[24]

God spoke to Moses, Abraham, Elijah, Paul and others, and there is no reason to think that He does not speak today. He speaks through prophets, visions, dreams or an audible voice, but primarily through His word. In fact, the Word of God is the product of the Holy Spirit, because He moved the holy men to write what we read today in the Bible.[25] Often when He speaks, He will lead us back to His Word to confirm and verify that it was He who spoke. A voice or a word that speaks contrary to His Word did not come from Him. The fact, however, that a word is unusual does not mean that God did not send it. He will verify His Word, especially if asked to do so.

The more one is conscious of being forgiven freely, the more he loves

How does one hear the voice of God? One individual on two different occasions, after losing money and her glasses, said she heard "something" tell her to look in her purse. In both cases she actually remembered responding that she had looked in the purse before and did not find either item. The voice or thought that entered her mind said again, "Look in your purse." When she did, she found both items.[26] In areas as seemingly small and insignificant as losing a few dollars or a pair of spectacles, God wants to speak to his believers so that they can become accustomed not only to hear, but to obey His voice. This is how the Spirit of God leads a believer.

On a personal note, I began to notice as I drove home from a church that I served as Pastor many years ago I would receive a sense or unction about which way to turn

[24] 1 Samuel 3:1-14

[25] 2 Peter 1:19-21

[26] My go out to Special thanks to Octavia Cormack for her experiences that found her way into this book.

to find a parking space. For weeks, I would come to the corner where the decisive turn would have to be made to park on one side of the street or on the other. Each night, I became more and more attuned to the voice and never failed to find a space to park.

When Elijah ran to mount Horeb in fear of Jezebel's murderous threats, he encountered an earthquake, a windstorm, and a firestorm.[27] Yet, God was not in any of the spectacular displays of earth, wind and fire. He, rather, was in a still small voice or a gentle whisper.

Supernatural gifts do not prove that one is sent from or is a part of Christ's body

It is not that the Spirit has not been speaking. One may not have been listening or perhaps listening for the wrong sound or type of voice. One may have been listening to the wrong voice or, in the jumble of a noisy environment, could not distinguish His voice above the competing clamor within our thoughts.

Sometimes that voice reminds one of a scripture that has been read or heard. Other times it is a nudge or a sense to do or avoid something. Some call it an unction. One might even engage in a silent mental conversation with that thought or impression without realizing that they are engaging the God of heaven in conversation.

Personally, I have made it a practice to communicate silently with God. According to the word only God searches the heart and the thoughts.[28] Therefore, I do not believe that the enemy can read one's mind. While the Devil can make an educated guess based on thousands of years of studying human psychology, only God knows exactly what one is thinking. By engaging the Lord in my thought-life, I have come to distinguish between the voice of God, my own thoughts and the lying and deceptive suggestions

[27] 1 Kings 19:9-13
[28] Jeremiah 17:10

of the enemy. This makes the study of the word essential so that one can distinguish between the Spirit of God and the spirit of Lucifer.[29]

All of the great leaders of the scriptures at some point early in their journey with God, found themselves alone with Him. Moses went to Midian to tend sheep. David also tended his father's sheep. Jesus went into the wilderness. Paul went to Arabia. Among many of the things that God was accomplishing in this isolation was the fine-tuning of their capacity to hear His voice. Often, Jesus would send the crowd and the disciples away and go into the mountain to commune with the Father alone.

This is an entirely new, different and unique life

Communing is two-way communication. It is praying or talking to God and listening for the response. The walk of the Spirit is communing continually with the Father through the Spirit. If Jesus lives in the believer, then that believer will walk even as He walked, and commune even as He communed.

As we learn to listen to the voice of the Spirit, He becomes the arbitrator between right and wrong; what to do and what not to do. The believer is led by the Spirit of God. Those that operated by the law interpreted for themselves how to relate to each precept and principle. Walking in the Spirit, however, means that the Spirit, who searches the intents of men's hearts, personally gives specific guidance and instruction to that individual. This means it becomes God that works in us both to will and to do of His good pleasure.[30]

An example of this was shown when Anninias and Saphira misrepresented their offering before Peter. He said that they "lied to the Holy Ghost."[31] The apostle Peter

---

[29] See Hebrews 5:13-14
[30] Philippians 2:13
[31] Acts 5:3

knew it because the Spirit revealed it to him. The Spirit not only gave the instruction and examined their motives, but He also knew their plans. Their hypocrisy and lying to appear generous and to impress others was abhorrent to God. It was the yeast of the Pharisees that Jesus warned about.[32] Under the law this scheme might have worked, but not in the realm of the Spirit. The consequence of this kind of disrespectful behavior in the presence of the Spirit was both immediate and severe.

Freedom from Fear and Condemnation

The word says that when the Anninias and Saphira incident took place "great fear seized "all of the believers. This word fear is often misunderstood. As God thundered His covenant with the Israelites, the Ten Commandments, from Mount Sinai, the people trembled with fear.[33] Moses, on the other hand, spoke of the fear of God being with them to keep from sinning. One definition of fear is being afraid of harm, danger, pain or punishment. Another definition of fear is a sense of awe and respect. The fear of the Lord is an awe and respect for Him that actually draws one to Him rather than giving the desire to run away from and cower in terror of Him. It could be compared to the reaction of a small child to a loving father. Even though the father might be an awesome and formidable presence, the child is drawn to his strong, powerful, yet protective embrace. The multitude in the wilderness ran from God, but Moses drew near to God. The people were afraid of God, but Moses feared the Lord. The fear of the Lord seized the believers after the incident with Anninias and Saphira. The believers drew near to the Lord out of

[32] Luke 12:1
[33] See Exodus 20:18-21

loving awe and respect resulting in rapid growth in the body of Christ.[34]

The motivation to obey God and His Spirit is not based on fear. We have not been given the spirit of fear.[35] The motivation of all religion that is based on the flesh and human effort is fear. The motivation of the new covenant believer, however, is love.[36] The only thing that counts is faith that works by love.[37]

Jesus obeyed the Father, not because he was afraid of Him, but because He loved to do what His father asked Him to do. It was His joy. He loved righteousness and hated iniquity.[38] If Christ is dwelling in the believer by the Spirit of God, that motivation will also be manifested.

The believer, because of dying with Christ, is free from the condemnation and penalty of sin. Yet, because His Spirit dwells within, that believer obeys. This is not from fear, but from love. He is free from the law and its condemnation because God no longer counts their sins against them, but he doesn't use his freedom as a license to sin. Even though he is free, he walks in obedience even as Jesus walked because the Son of God through the Spirit of God lives within him. He has awakened to righteousness,[39] just as Jesus was awakened from the grave. The believer lives by the Spirit and his desire, like Jesus', is to please the Father.

---

[34] An excellent and invaluable resource on this subject is The Fear of the Lord by John Bevere, Strang Communications, Lake Mary, FL 1997

[35] 2 Timothy 1:7 (KJV)

[36] 1 John 4:16-18

[37] Galatians 5:6

[38] See Psalm 45:7 and Hebrews 1:8-9

[39] 1 Corinthians 15:34 (KJV)

The Key Difference Between the Covenants

This highlights the major difference between the old and the new covenant. The shift is from outward behavior to inward motivations. The law could only point out what one did. The Spirit of God addresses what one wants to do because, once again, it is God who works in us both to will and to do of His good pleasure.[40]

Under the new covenant God specifically promised He would provide for every aspect of the terms of the agreement. He said, "I will put my laws in their heart and mind and I will forgive their wickedness and remember their sins no more. They will all know Me, from the least to the greatest." In other words, they will all hear His voice.[41]

The outcome of the New Covenant is dependent not on the believer's faithfulness, but rather on God's. This is clearly seen in the experience of Abram when God confirmed His covenant with him. In Genesis 15, as mentioned earlier, the Lord put Abram to sleep as a smoking firepot and a lamp passed through the bloody pathway of split animal carcasses. God, who is a consuming fire,[42] traveled through the pieces. What about the lamp? The Bible points to the Word as to one's feet and a light to one's path.[43] Jesus refers to Himself as the light of the world[44] and the Word of God[45] as two of His many titles. What happened, as mentioned in the previous chapter, while Abram slept, the Father and the Son, symbolized by

These born again believers are led and guided by the Spirit

[40] Philippians 2:13 (KJV)
[41] Jeremiah 31:34 and Hebrews 8:7-14, See also John 10:1-18
[42] John 1:12
[43] Psalm 119:105
[44] John 1:4-5, 9:43
[45] John 1:1-14 and Revelation 19:13

the lamp and a smoking fire pot, covenanted on behalf of Abram and his descendants. God covenanted with Himself promising and assuring Abram that He would fulfill His commitments to him.

In Isaiah's prophecies God declared that He made His Servant to be a covenant for the people.[46] In the book of the Psalms the Lord declared and swore an oath regarding His commitment to Our Lord's kingdom and priesthood.[47] These covenants are between God and Christ; The Father and His only begotten Son.

The faithfulness that is counted on to guarantee this new covenant, then is God's and Christ's. The assurance that the promises and provisions will be manifest and come to pass is based on the reliability of God to keeping His Word. Jesus, understanding this, said in His prayer of John 17 that He sanctified Himself so that His followers and disciples would be truly sanctified.[48] Even if the believer is faithless, He remains faithful.[49] Everything hinges on His faithfulness. That is what counts.

In the same passage Paul wrote to Timothy, "If you disown Him He will disown you."[50] This means that once one has believed and received Christ as a gift from the Father, one can squander and lose it (or Him). This disowning is more than a mistake, weakness or shortcoming, because provision for missing of the mark has been supplied to the believer through Jesus. He is also the believer's Advocate or legal representative with the Father.[51] To disown means to personally repudiate Christ, then position oneself in direct opposition to Him and line up with the enemy. It is a complete denial of who He is as revealed by the Spirit of God. This can

[46] Isaiah 42:6, 49:8
[47] Psalm 110
[48] John 17:19
[49] 2 Timothy 2:13
[50] 2 Timothy 2:12b
[51] 1 John 2:1

also be done by disregarding the voice of the Spirit and yielding to the control of Satan by repeatedly responding to his suggestions to satisfy the flesh. It need not be some heinous or grotesque tendency. Pride, envy, greed, hatred or any area of the flesh will yield the same results. Judas, who walked with Jesus, yielded himself to the enemy and ultimately, under the demonic influence of despair and despondency, hanged himself. Yet Peter, who denied Christ three times, found his way back into fellowship with Him. Jesus said that all manner of sin and blasphemy would be forgiven among men.[52] Without question, one can wander away, but once one resubmits to Christ, He will receive him back.

The goal of the New Covenant is to produce sons of God. New internal motivations are implanted in the believer making a brand new creation;[53] to make a bad tree into a good one.[54] A good tree produces good fruit. Its nature and internal chemistry makes that a certainty. This is God's solution in the New Covenant.

The believer's nature is replaced with one that loves righteousness, hates iniquity[55] and delights to do the will of the Father.[56] It is neither practiced nor developed. It is supernaturally implanted by faith. Believers, alerted by their poverty of spirit and hunger and thirst for righteousness are subsequently filled. The internal motives of hate and lust, for example, are identified as problems long before the actual acts of murder and adultery are committed. The righteousness of those who put their trust in Christ exceeds that of those, such as the scribes and Pharisees, who focused only on external conduct and law keeping.[57]

---

[52] Matthew 12:31a and Mark 3:28
[53] 2 Corinthians 5:17
[54] Matthew 12:33
[55] See Hebrews 1:8-9
[56] Psalm 45:7
[57] See Matthew 5

Those who are under the New Covenant, who are led by and listen to the Spirit of God, are daily, hourly and moment-by-moment guided by His prompting. Their focus is to hear God's voice and obey Him.

The Struggle with Flesh

This is not to suggest that there is no struggle. That struggle is not with sin (although it involves temptation and transgression), but with the inner tug of the flesh. Paul outlines it in his letter to the Romans. From chapters one through three he establishes that all Jews and gentiles alike, are guilty of sin. He summarizes this by writing "All have sinned and come short of the glory."[58] Then, he reveals God's solution for sin in chapters four through six. It is in this section that he discusses how God declares the wicked to be righteous.[59]

It is in chapter seven, after the person is declared righteous, that he introduces a new struggle. By faith the believer has received forgiveness through the Blood of Christ. He has been exonerated from guilt and any penalty by his death with Christ. His old nature has been buried with Christ. But, as Paul writes, he finds this internal conflict between his mind, which wants to follow God, and the law of sin in his members (flesh) that wants to do the opposite. This is where the real battle is waged; between the desires of the flesh and the renewed mind. In effect, this battle is between the Spirit of Christ, which loves righteousness and hates iniquity, and the tendencies of the flesh tempted to be reasserted, revived and resurrected by the suggestions of the enemy. Whoever the believer yields to will rule his heart and mind. Ultimately, Paul thanked God for Christ who delivers him from this struggle and

[58] Romans 3:21

[59] Romans 5:4

"body of death"[60] "for greater is He that is in us than he that is in the world."[61]

This walk requires truth in the inward parts.[62] This is an honesty with one's self and with God on an intimate level. It is at this level of honesty and openness that any lingering struggles with the flesh are discussed with the Father. This is where and how the Spirit of God wants this communion to be. "They all will know Me," He says,"from the least of them to the greatest."[63] We will know even as we are known.[64] The communion of the believer is in their innermost being where nothing is out of bounds or hidden from the Father.

In the old covenant only the high priests were allowed to enter the most holy place of the old covenant sanctuary where the presence of God was, and that happened only once a year during the Day of Atonement. Now, the body of every believer is the temple of the Holy Ghost. One continually lives in His presence through the Spirit of Christ. God now dwells in every believer by faith. We have this treasure in jars of clay (our bodies) showing that this all surpassing power is from God and not us.[65]

The Fruit of the Spirit

Remember, flesh and sins are buried, symbolized by baptism. The Father places his Son in the believer by the Spirit to lead and guide him and also to quicken or give life to his new walk.

In Ephesians 2:10 the Spirit says that all of the good works of believers were prepared in advance for them. The

[60] Romans 7:24 (KJV)
[61] I John 4:4
[62] Psalm 51:6
[63] Jeremiah 31:34 and Hebrews 8:11
[64] 1 Corinthians 13:12
[65] 2 Corinthians 4:7

life that the believer now lives is not his or produced by him. It is Christ's life placed there by the Spirit of God. Every believer who walks in the Spirit by faith has it. It is unmistakable. It can not be counterfeited or faked. It is the royal law that the Spirit spoke through James.[66] It is the identifying mark that Jesus said would distinguish His disciples from everyone else. Only the Spirit of God can produce it in a believer.[67]

This fruit of the Spirit is love. This love is expressed in patience, kindness, gentleness, peace, goodness, faithfulness, joy and self-control.[68] It does not envy, delight in evil, keep record of wrongs or boast. It is not proud, easily angered, self seeking or rude. It protects, always trusts, rejoices in the truth, hopes and perseveres.[69] Those under its power love both their enemies and those that persecute them.[70] Only the Spirit of Christ can produce that kind of fruit.

The law is good at pointing out wrongs and transgressions, but it could not do anything about the sinful nature. It could produce individuals who worked diligently to avoid certain behaviors and actions, but it could not produce love in the heart or the spirit of self sacrifice. The Father wasn't trying to get people to act a certain way. He wanted sons and daughters who love Him and would allow His Spirit to live in them by faith.

---

[66] James 2:8
[67] John 13:34-35
[68] Galatians 5:23
[69] 1 Corinthians 13:4-7
[70] Matthew 5:11, 43-48 and Luke 6:27-36

Where the Love for God Comes From

They love Him because, for those who have discovered what He has given freely through His Son, they realize that while they were in their sins or even before they were born that He demonstrated His love for them in a tangible way by sending His Son.

Jesus was an invited guest for dinner held by a prominent Pharisee. A woman from town who was not invited to the dinner approached Jesus. Everyone knew she had a spotted reputation. She wet his feet with her tears, wiped them with her hair, kissed and anointed them with some extremely expensive perfume. As the whispering, stares and raised eyebrows began to fill the room, Jesus corrected their erroneous perceptions with a parable.

He told the story of two men who owed money to a money lender. One owed almost two years' pay. The other owed about two months' wages. Both had their debts cancelled. He asked, "Which of them loved him more?" The obvious answer was the one who owed more. Then, motioning to the woman, He pointed out that her acts were similar to those of the one who owed a huge debt because of sin, but was forgiven of them all. For those who had been forgiven much and their debt was completely paid, they would love much.[71]

Love for the Lord Jesus flows like a rushing river after a flood from those who are forgiven and know it. For those who work for their pardon, there is little energy left to love. They feel as if they deserve forgiveness; they have worked for it. However, for those who received it freely, without price or effort on their own, tears filled with grateful joy and love will overflow. The more one is conscious of being forgiven freely, the more one loves.

Jesus' name literally means Jehovah is Savior. It is the Father that Jesus points us to as the One who should be

[71] Luke 7:40-47

thanked for what was done for us. Jesus also loves the Father and, as His life is expressed through the believer, that love will be evidenced more and more.

In His third of three last day parables recorded in Matthew, Jesus revealed the criteria that will be used to separate those who were His (sheep) from those who were not (goats).[72] The behaviors described were not covered in the law that Moses brought down from the mountain on tablets of stone. They were, however, acts of generosity, kindness and self-sacrifice. In short, they were acts of love. Interestingly, those represented as sheep were unaware of their behaviors. They asked, "When did we do these things?" They were not trying to impress, perform a duty, do something for a reward or to fulfill an obligation. They were simply doing what they were being led to do and they thought nothing of it. They were simply accustomed to following the Spirit's prompting and operating in the nature of Christ implanted within them. They were the acts of those who are filled with the Spirit of God and were manifesting His fruit; love. Against such there is no law.[73]

The Gifts of the Spirit of God

The Holy Spirit also gives gifts to believers. These gifts empower them for ministry and witness. The Holy Spirit distributes each gift as He chooses. The gifts include supernatural capabilities as well as some seemingly ordinary abilities. All are necessary for the body of Christ to function together effectively and efficiently. The offices of Apostle, Prophet, Evangelist, Pastor and Teacher are gifts of the Spirit.[74] These gifted offices edify the body of

[72] Matthew 25:31-46

[73] Galatians 5:23

[74] 1 Corinthians 12:27-28 and Ephesians 4:11-13

believers, teach and prepare the body for ministry, bring unity into the fellowship and help the body to mature into the fullness of Christ.

The gifts of healing, miraculous power, prophecy, tongues, interpretation of tongues, discerning of spirits, wisdom and knowledge are also given by the Holy Spirit.[75] Faith, serving, encouraging, contributing and leadership are also listed as gifts of the Spirit.[76] While some of these gifts seem less spectacular than others, they, nonetheless are not only important, but vital to the body.

One thing should be noted. Gifts and callings are "without repentance."[77] In other words, God gives gifts to individuals as He wills and the person with the gift does not have to be a faithful believer to operate in their gift. Many, Jesus said, would perform many miracles, prophesy and cast out demons in His name, yet He never knew them. Ultimately He calls them "evildoers."

Supernatural gifts do not prove that one is sent from or is a part of Christ's body. Supernatural manifestations or signs can be faked and duplicated. The magicians and sorcerers in Pharaoh's court performed a few of the plagues in Egypt.[78] While the things that mark an apostle, signs, wonders and miracles,[79] Satan can and will produce these as well.[80]

Only one thing, however, identifies His followers: the fruit of the Spirit, which is love. Faith that works by love by God's Spirit is what counts.[81] Every believer who has received Christ by faith will have this fruit, because God said so in His Word. They listen to His voice and walk by His Spirit. And those who are led by His Spirit are the Sons of God.[82]

---

[75] 1 Corinthians 12:4-11

[76] Romans 12:3-8

[77] Romans 11:29 (KJV)

[78] Exodus 7:11, 22, 8:7

[79] 2 Corinthians 12:12

[80] 2 Thessalonians 2:9

[81] Galatians 5:6b

[82] Romans 8:14

Chapter 6

The Gift of Adoption

For if you live according to the sinful nature, you will die; but if by the Spirit you put to death the misdeeds of the body, you will live, because those who are led by the Spirit of God are sons of God. For you did not receive a spirit that makes you a slave again to fear, but you received the Spirit of sonship. And by him we cry, "Abba, Father." The Spirit himself testifies with our spirit that we are God's children. Now if we are children, then we are heirs—heirs of God and co-heirs with Christ, if indeed we share in his sufferings in order that we may also share in his glory (Romans 8:13-17).

For those God foreknew he also predestined to be conformed to the likeness of his Son, that he might be the firstborn among many brothers (Romans 8:29).

What, then, shall we say in response to this? If God is for us, who can be against us? He who did not spare his own Son, but gave him up for us all—how will he not also, along with him, graciously give us all things? Who will bring any charge against those whom God has chosen? It is God who justifies. Who is he that condemns? Christ Jesus, who died—more than that, who was raised to life—is at the right hand of God and is also interceding for us. Who shall separate us from the love of Christ? Shall trouble or hardship or persecution or famine or nakedness or danger or sword? As it is written: "For your sake we face death all day long; we are considered as sheep to be slaughtered." No, in all these things we are more than conquerors through him who loved us. For I am convinced that neither death nor life, neither angels nor demons, neither the present nor the future, nor any powers, neither height nor depth, nor anything else in all creation, will be able to separate us from the love of God that is in Christ Jesus our Lord (Romans 8:31-39).

How great is the love the Father has lavished on us, that we should be called children of God! And that is what we are! The reason the world does not know us is that it did not know him. Dear friends, now we are children of God, and what we will be has not yet been made known. But we know that when he appears, we shall be like him, for we shall see him as he is (1 John 3:1-2).

You are all sons of God through faith in Christ Jesus, for all of you who were baptized into Christ have clothed yourselves with Christ. There is neither Jew nor Greek, slave nor free, male nor female, for you are all one in Christ Jesus. If you belong to Christ, then you are Abraham's seed, and heirs according to the promise (Galatians 3:26-29).

What I am saying is that as long as the heir is a child, he is no different from a slave, although he owns the whole estate. He is subject to guardians and trustees until the time set by his father. So also, when we were children, we were in slavery under the basic principles of the world. But when the time had fully come, God sent his Son, born of a woman, born under law, to redeem those under law, that we might receive the full rights of sons. Because you are sons, God sent the Spirit of his Son into our hearts, the Spirit who calls out, "Abba, Father." So you are no longer a slave, but a son; and since you are a son, God has made you also an heir (Galatians 4:1-7).

Jesus said, "Do not hold on to me, for I have not yet returned to the Father. Go instead to my brothers and tell them, 'I am returning to my Father and your Father, to my God and your God'" (John 20:17).

For those God foreknew he also predestined to be conformed to the likeness of his Son, that he might be the firstborn among many brothers (Romans 8:29).

As the week of Creation was winding down, God, who had spoken everything into existence, spoke to Himself. "Let us make man in our image and in our likeness and let them rule."[1] He carefully molded, formed and sculpted the moist clay, perhaps by a riverbed, into a man. After He was satisfied with His workmanship, God approached the nostrils of the lifeless form, and gently blew. The clay morphed into flesh from the life-giving contact with its Creator. The chest of the magnificent statue expanded for the first time. It breathed and the eyes opened. The inanimate clay, now a living and breathing man, looked face to face for the first time at his Father.

God, then, took the man and instructed him about his environment, his home, his responsibilities and his relationship to all of the things He created. He commanded the man to assume authority over what he had been freely given and also specifically instructed him what to avoid and why. He gave him the responsibility to guard and keep the realm over which he had authority.

As long as the man yielded himself to God, all that God gave him remain unchanged

As God concluded His instructions, He took the man by the hand, like a father leading his son, and walked him, possibly to the same exact spot where he was first formed. God kneeled down, and one after another He formed the various animals of the field and the birds of the air and brought each molded form to the man.[2] As the man spoke the name he chose for the creature, the lifeless clay form came to life and flew, loped, galloped or scampered away. Man was being taught to act and speak like his Father. As

---

[1] Genesis 1:26

[2] Genesis 2:19-20

the Son, who would later be known as a life given Spirit[3] would later say, "I do what I see my Father do."[4]

The man recognized that each animal and bird had a mate; male and female. Yet, he had none. As he looked to his Maker as if to ask "Why," God caused a deep sleep to befall the man and made the female out of substance taken from man's side. After the man was awakened, God walked His newest creation to Adam. He waited on His son's words. Adam declared her name, accepted her as his mate and they became one flesh. Together, under the authority of God in the order He set up and with the commands given the man, they would rule and exercise dominion over all that He had created.

> When I consider your heavens,
> the work of your fingers,
> the moon and the stars,
> which you have set in place,
> what is man that you are mindful of him,
> the son of man that you care for him?
> You made him a little lower than the heavenly beings
> and crowned him with glory and honor.
> You made him ruler over the works of your hands;
> you put everything under his feet:
> all flocks and herds,
> and the beasts of the field,
> the birds of the air,
> and the fish of the sea,
> all that swim the paths of the seas.[5]

Notice that all of the instructions were given to the man. Although man and woman were equal and would rule together, the man came first. He came first and was from the ground, while the woman came afterward and

---

[3] 1 Corinthians 15:45

[4] John 5:19

[5] Psalm 8:3-8

was made from material from his side. He was given the instructions and commands from God. He also named the animals as well as woman. He was held responsible and his actions determined the destiny of the woman and everything else that was under his authority. That included the plants, tree and animals.

When later the man chose to listen to a voice other than his Father, everything was plunged into rebellion. Whoever you yield yourself to as an obedient servant the Word of God teaches, you are his servant and in effect he is your Lord.[6] As long as the man yielded himself to God, all that God gave him remained unchanged. He had dominion, power, authority, honor, his every need was met, the environment submitted to his will including animals who obeyed his commands. However, when Adam listened to Satan, he lost the scepter of rulership and his inheritance.

God lost something too. He lost a son.

God lost something too. He lost a son. He lost the daily fellowship of an inquiring, questioning and inquisitive being created to be like Him. A being, who like Himself, worked and rested, recreated, exercised authority and had volition: a will, the power to choose. God had created "another speaking spirit"[7] made after his likeness and image. Fortunately, Adam's rebellion did not take God by surprise. He had a plan to redeem and restore His lost son and those that were trapped by his choice.

By the actions of Adam all men became the object of God's wrath, but He sent His Son and we believers have peace with God. Man was condemned to death. The law that came later reminded man of his guilt and demanded the penalty of death because of the multitude of individual

[6] Romans 6:16

[7] The Chumash 11th Edition Menorah Publications Ltd., Brooklyn NY 1993, 1999, 2000, 2001, 2002, 2003, page 11

transgressions or acts of sin. But God sent His uniquely begotten Son and the death He died was the death Adam and all after him should have died. He also freed them from the influence of sinful flesh.

God's desire was to have many sons like His One and Only Son

Man had no power to walk in God's righteous ways, but God put His Son into man by His Spirit to enable and empower him to walk even as He walked. But what about the lofty position of dominion and authority that man once had. How would he ever find his way back to that?

A Story of Restoration

Jesus told the story of a man who had two sons.[8] The youngest, who was too impatient to wait until the death of the Father to inherit his portion of the estate, demanded it right away. Upon receiving his share, he packed his belongings and headed for the bright lights and the big city. Quickly, his money ran out and so did all of his new-found friends. Finally, he found himself alone and hired out to a man who gave this Jewish boy the worst job he could find for him—caring for pigs.

When the young man, as the Bible says, came to himself, he resolved to see if his father would hire him. "At least" he thought, "people that work for my father do better than this. I have wasted my inheritance and am no longer worthy to be called your son, but let me be a hired hand."

He arrived home and before he could begin his prepared speech, his father hid his son's shameful and untidy appearance with a robe. He put shoes on his feet,because only slaves go around barefoot. Finally, he placed a ring, perhaps with the family seal or crest on it, on his finger. He

[8] Luke 15:11-32

was restored to his proper place as a son. His inheritance was restored.

In the book of Hebrews one of the aspects of death is mentioned in connection with the reading of a will.[9] The writer stated that a will is not placed in force until the death of the one who made it. After the death, however, the provisions of the will are enforced. The inheritance of the believer is assured, restored and now available to the believer because of the death of Christ.

One Seed Became Many Seeds

God's plan for the restoration of His sons was to replace His first son,[10] Adam, with another and anyone who received this last Adam by faith would be adopted or, more appropriately, restored to sonship. Jesus was this last Adam. The Word of God assures believers that they are all sons of God through faith in Christ Jesus. All who received Him, to those who believed in His name, He gave the right to become the children or sons of God, children born not of natural descent, nor of human decision or a husband's will, but born of God.[11]

By accepting one's death by faith with Christ, the connection to Adam and the results of his rebellion against God's authority was severed. The Father connected the believer to His Son's dominion and Kingdom. Therefore, since He is born from above, the believer is also born from above and shares in His throne and dominion.

Jesus said "unless a kernel of wheat falls to the ground and dies, it remains only a single seed. But if it dies, it

[9] Hebrews 9:16-17
[10] See Luke 3:38
[11] John 1:12-13

produces many seeds."[12] God's desire was to have many sons like His one and only Son.

This is not to be interpreted that believers are immediately sinless in their behavior. Jesus was born of a woman and under the law, yet He was different from us. His Father was not like any ordinary child's. He was born by the Holy Ghost. He was sinless, meaning He had no inclination for sin or a sinful nature as every other child was born with. He was not connected in any way to the fallen Adam, for all bloodlines, which include those traits, weaknesses and sinful characteristics, descend from the father. Jesus' Father, however, was God, just like Adam before he fell.

The Bible states that anyone who claims to be sinless or does not sin is a liar.[13] Dying with Jesus by faith has paid all of the believer's sins. His sins are not imputed or counted against him because of his Advocate (defense attorney) representing him before the ultimate Judge.

Falling Short of the Glory

The Bible says all have sinned and come or fall short of His glory.[14] Again, by faith in Jesus' shed blood and His death, the believer's sin problem is solved and, by the Spirit of Christ being placed within, he has risen to walk in a new life. What then is this "glory" that many fall short of?

Throughout Jesus' life, the Father would audibly express His pleasure with His Son. His statements amount to boasting about how pleased He was in Him, just as a proud Father bragging about His Son would do. What Jesus did is what He saw the Father do.[15] He

[12] John 12:24

[13] 1 John 1:18

[14] Romans 3:23

[15] John 5:19, 8:28-29

said what the Father told Him to say.[16] It was His desire and pleasure to do His Father's will. As a result, the Father, through the Spirit, empowered His every word and action.

Jesus spoke and acted with the authority and dominion of the Son of God. This title has nothing to do with Him being the second person in the Godhead. Remember, Adam was God's son as well[17] and he was given all authority and dominion in the earth. He lost it. Jesus reclaimed it. Now we have access to that authority and dominion through Him.

The "glory" is walking and operating in the dominion and authority of a son and daughter of God through Jesus. Those who walk daily with their faith and trust in the Gift that the Father has freely given, are the sons (and daughters) of God with all of the rights and privileges that come with it.

One stormy night, while trying to cross a lake, this reality was exemplified.[18] Peter asked Jesus, who chose to walk on the water instead of the conventional method of using a boat, for permission to join Him for a stroll on the stormy lake. His wish was granted and, for the first time, Peter experienced dominion over the elements through his faith in one word from Jesus' mouth: "Come."

Jesus spoke to the winds and the waves and these elements of nature obeyed Him. Demons bowed before Him and pleaded for His indulgence. Sickness followed His specific instructions. Water became wine. A sack lunch became a feast for thousands. Death was not exempt from His command. He said that greater than these would those who followed Him also do.[19]

The apostles caught the vision and like Jesus healed the sick, raised the dead, commanded demons and

---

[16] John 12:49-50

[17] Luke 8:38

[18] Matthew 14:22-33

[19] John 14:11-12

walked in the authority of sons of God through Christ Jesus. Paul wrote that believers in Christ Jesus were no longer slaves or servants, but sons and joint-heirs with Christ.[20] They are seated by faith with Christ in heavenly places,[21] with Jesus being the firstborn of many brothers.[22]

Often during His ministry Jesus referred to God as "My Father." Yet after His resurrection as He tried to escape Mary's prolonged embrace, he said, "I am returning to my Father and your Father, to my God and your God."[23] He had successfully retrieved what Adam had lost and anyone who is connected to Him by faith is restored to the full stature of sonship through Him.

The Believer's New Focus

When the primary focus is sin rather than the good news of the Gift of the Father in Christ, the glory of operating as a son or daughter of God is neither anticipated nor experienced by believers. This, just as everything else from the Father, is part of the Gift He has freely given in His Son. It is not earned or worked for. It is received and maintained by faith. The same way the believer received Christ (by faith), he continues to live in Him.[24] Nothing else pleases God.

What does it mean to be a son of God and a joint-heir with Christ? It means unlimited resources and access to someone who has power and authority over everything from the smallest atom to the galaxies of space. His dominion includes authority over life and death. He is not

[20] Romans 8:17 and Galatians 3:29

[21] Ephesians 2:6

[22] Romans 8:29-30

[23] John 20:17

[24] Colossians 2:6

just God. He is Father, or Daddy. We can cry unto Him, "Abba" which is Aramaic for Daddy.[25]

For those whose daddies are gone, this means more than can be expressed in words. Those shoulders that could be cried on, the stable presence, the provider, the one to go to for advice is available and nothing can take Him away.[26]

As the believer grows and matures, more and more authority and dominion will be expressed in his or her life. This will be proportionate to the gifts given by the Spirit. Yet all of His children will walk and talk like sons and daughters of God. All creation groans in anticipation of the revelation of these sons of God.[27]

This is not new. There were men whose words God would not allow to fall to the ground[28] and whose prayers God answered with fire, drought, rain and earthquakes. That authority will be manifested again and again as men and women embrace what the Father has given freely in His Son by faith, especially as His second coming approaches.

By faith, sins are atoned by His blood, there is no condemnation of the law and the power of the flesh is broken by dying with Him. The Spirit of God has been implanted in the heart and Christ lives on the inside. The sonship lost by Adam is restored to its full status.

What, then, is our response to these things?

---

[25] Romans 8:16

[26] See Psalm 103:13

[27] Romans 8:19

[28] 1 Samuel 3:19

Chapter 7

Praise

What a wretched man I am! Who will rescue me from this body of death? Thanks be to God—through Jesus Christ our Lord! (Romans 7:24-25a).

Praise be to the God and Father of our Lord Jesus Christ, who has blessed us in the heavenly realms with every spiritual blessing in Christ. For he chose us in him before the creation of the world to be holy and blameless in his sight. In love he predestined us to be adopted as his sons through Jesus Christ, in accordance with his pleasure and will—to the praise of his glorious grace, which he has freely given us in the One he loves. In him we have redemption through his blood, the forgiveness of sins, in accordance with the riches of God's grace that he lavished on us with all wisdom and understanding. And he made known to us the mystery of his will according to his good pleasure, which he purposed in Christ, to be put into effect when the times will have reached their fulfillment—to bring all things in heaven and on earth together under one head, even Christ. In him we were also chosen, having been predestined according to the plan of him who works out everything in conformity with the purpose of his will, in order that we, who were the first to hope in Christ, might be for the praise of his glory. And you also were included in Christ when you heard the word of truth, the gospel of your salvation. Having believed, you were marked in him with a seal, the promised Holy Spirit, who is a deposit guaranteeing our inheritance until the redemption of those who are God's possession—to the praise of his glory. For this reason, ever since I heard about your faith in the Lord Jesus and your love for all the saints, I have not stopped giving thanks for you, remembering you in my prayers. I keep asking that the God of our Lord Jesus Christ, the glorious Father, may give you the Spirit of wisdom and revelation, so that you may know him better. I pray also that the eyes of your heart may be enlightened in order that you may know the hope to which he has called you, the riches of his glorious inheritance in the saints, and his incomparably great power for us who believe. That power is like the working of his mighty strength, which he exerted in Christ when he raised him from the dead and seated him at his right hand in the heavenly realms, far above all rule and authority, power and dominion, and every title that can be given, not only in the present age but also in the one to come. And God placed all things under his feet and appointed him to be head over everything for the church, which is his body, the fullness of him who fills everything in every way (Ephesians 1:3-23).

We always thank God, the Father of our Lord Jesus Christ, when we pray for you, because we have heard of your faith in Christ Jesus and of the love you have for all the saints—the faith and love that spring from the hope that is stored up for you in heaven and that you have already heard about in the word of truth, the gospel that has come to you. All over the world this gospel is bearing fruit and growing, just as it has been doing among you since the day you heard it and understood God's grace in all its truth. You learned it from Epaphras, our dear fellow servant, who is a faithful minister of Christ on our behalf, and who also told us of your love in the Spirit. For this reason, since the day we heard about you, we have not stopped praying for you and asking God to fill you with the knowledge of his will through all spiritual wisdom and understanding. And we pray this in order that you may live a life worthy of the Lord and may please him in every way: bearing fruit in every good work, growing in the knowledge of God, being strengthened with all power according to his glorious might so that you may have great endurance and patience, and joyfully giving thanks to the Father, who has qualified you to share in the inheritance of the saints in the kingdom of light. For he has rescued us from the dominion of darkness and brought us into the kingdom of the Son he loves, in whom we have redemption, the forgiveness of sins. He is the image of the invisible God, the firstborn over all creation. For by him all things were created: things in heaven and on earth, visible and invisible, whether thrones or powers or rulers or authorities; all things were created by him and for him. He is before all things, and in him all things hold together. And he is the head of the body, the church; he is the beginning and the firstborn from among the dead, so that in everything he might have the supremacy. For God was pleased to have all his fullness dwell in him, and through him to reconcile to himself all things, whether things on earth or things in heaven, by making peace through his blood, shed on the cross (Colossians 1:3-20).

"'After this I will return and rebuild David's fallen tent. Its ruins I will rebuild, and I will restore it, that the remnant of men may seek the Lord, and all the Gentiles who bear my name, says the Lord, who does these things' that have been known for ages (Acts 15:16-18).

As the ark of the Lord was entering the City of David, Michal daughter of Saul watched from a window. And when she saw King David leaping and dancing before the Lord, she despised him in her heart. They brought the ark of the Lord and set it in its place inside the tent that David had pitched for it, and David sacrificed burnt offerings and fellowship offerings before the Lord. After he had finished sacrificing the burnt offerings and fellowship offerings, he blessed the people in the name of the Lord Almighty. Then he gave a loaf of bread, a cake of dates and a cake of raisins to each person in the whole crowd of Israelites, both men and women. And all the people went to their homes (2 Samuel 6:16-19).

So David and the elders of Israel and the commanders of units of a thousand went to bring up the ark of the covenant of the Lord from the house of Obed-Edom, with rejoicing. Because God had helped the Levites who were carrying the ark of the covenant of the Lord, seven bulls and seven rams were sacrificed. Now David was clothed in a robe of fine linen, as were all the Levites who were carrying the ark, and as were the singers, and Kenaniah, who was in charge of the singing of the choirs. David also wore a linen ephod. So all Israel brought up the ark of the covenant of the Lord with shouts, with the sounding of rams' horns and trumpets, and of cymbals, and the playing of lyres and harps. As the ark of the covenant of the Lord was entering the City of David, Michal daughter of Saul watched from a window. And when she saw King David dancing and celebrating, she despised him in her heart.

They brought the ark of God and set it inside the tent that David had pitched for it, and they presented burnt offerings and fellowship offerings before God. After David had finished sacrificing the burnt offerings and fellowship offerings, he blessed the people in the name of the Lord. Then he gave a loaf of bread, a cake of dates and a cake of raisins to each Israelite man and woman.

He appointed some of the Levites to minister before the ark of the Lord, to make petition, to give thanks, and to praise the Lord, the God of Israel: Asaph was the chief, Zechariah second, then Jeiel, Shemiramoth, Jehiel, Mattithiah, Eliab, Benaiah, Obed-Edom and Jeiel. They were to play the lyres and harps, Asaph was to sound the cymbals, and Benaiah and Jahaziel the priests were to blow the trumpets regularly before the ark of the covenant of God (1 Chronicles 15:25-16:6).

David left Asaph and his associates before the ark of the covenant of the Lord to minister there regularly, according to each day's requirements. He also left Obed-Edom and his sixty-eight associates to minister with them. Obed-Edom son of Jeduthun, and also Hosah, were gatekeepers. David left Zadok the priest and his fellow priests before the tabernacle of the Lord at the high place in Gibeon to present burnt offerings to the Lord on the altar of burnt offering regularly, morning and evening, in accordance with everything written in the Law of the Lord, which he had given Israel. With them were Heman and Jeduthun and the rest of those chosen and designated by name to give thanks to the Lord, "for his love endures forever." Heman and Jeduthun were responsible for the sounding of the trumpets and cymbals and for the playing of the other instruments for sacred song. The sons of Jeduthun were stationed at the gate (1 Chronicles 16:37-42).

Rejoice in the Lord always. I will say it again: Rejoice! Let your gentleness be evident to all. The Lord is near. Do not be anxious about anything, but in everything, by prayer and petition, with thanksgiving, present your requests to God. And the peace of God, which transcends all understanding, will guard your hearts and your minds in Christ Jesus (Philippians 4:4-7).

After this I looked, and there before me was a door standing open in heaven. And the voice I had first heard speaking to me like a trumpet said, "Come up here, and I will show you what must take place after this." At once I was in the Spirit, and there before me was a throne in heaven with someone sitting on it. And the one who sat there had the appearance of jasper and carnelian. A rainbow, resembling an emerald, encircled the throne. Surrounding the throne were twenty-four other thrones, and seated on them were twenty-four elders. They were dressed in white and had crowns of gold on their heads. From the throne came flashes of lightning, rumblings and peals of thunder. Before the throne, seven lamps were blazing. These are the seven spirits of God. Also before the throne there was what looked like a sea of glass, clear as crystal. In the center, around the throne, were four living creatures, and they were covered with eyes, in front and in back. The first living creature was like a lion, the second was like an ox, the third had a face like a man, the fourth was like a flying eagle. Each of the four living creatures had six wings and was covered with eyes all around, even under his wings. Day and night they never stop saying:

"Holy, holy, holy
is the Lord God Almighty,
who was, and is, and is to come."

Whenever the living creatures give glory, honor and thanks to him who sits on the throne and who lives for ever and ever, the twenty-four elders fall down before him who sits on the throne, and worship him who lives for ever and ever. They lay their crowns before the throne and say: "You are worthy, our Lord and God, to receive glory and honor and power, for you created all things, and by your will they were created and have their being." Then I saw in the right hand of him who sat on the throne a scroll with writing on both sides and sealed with seven seals. And I saw a mighty angel proclaiming in a loud voice, "Who is worthy to break the seals and open the scroll?" But no one in heaven or on earth or under the earth could open the scroll or even look inside it. I wept and wept because no one was found who was worthy to open the scroll or look inside. Then one of the elders said to me, "Do not weep! See, the Lion of the tribe of Judah, the Root of David, has triumphed. He is able to open the scroll and its seven seals." Then I saw a Lamb, looking as if it had been slain, standing in the center of the throne, encircled by the four living creatures and the elders. He had seven horns and seven eyes, which are the seven spirits of God sent out into all the earth. He came and took the scroll from the right hand of him who sat on the throne. And when he had taken it, the four living creatures and the twenty-four elders fell down before the Lamb. Each one had a harp and they were holding golden bowls full of incense, which are the prayers of the saints. And they sang a new song:

"You are worthy to take the scroll and to open its seals, because you were slain, and with your blood you purchased men for God from every tribe and language and people and nation. You have made them to be a kingdom and priests to serve our God, and they will reign on the earth." Then I looked and heard the voice of many angels, numbering thousands upon thousands, and ten thousand times ten thousand. They encircled the throne and the living creatures and the elders. In a loud voice they sang:

"Worthy is the Lamb, who was slain,
to receive power and wealth and wisdom and strength
and honor and glory and praise!"

Then I heard every creature in heaven and on earth and under the earth and on the sea, and all that is in them, singing:

"To him who sits on the throne and to the Lamb
be praise and honor and glory and power,
for ever and ever!"

The four living creatures said, "Amen," and the elders fell down and worshiped.

Moments before one of Jesus' greatest miracles, He prayed. It is the prayer of a man who was confident. He was confident in His relationship built on years of constant communion. He was also confident in His Father's willingness to perform His Word and confident in His Father's ability to accomplish what is about to be attempted. He didn't beg or plead. He simply stated the facts that His faith stood on. He did not ask for what He already had. In fact, His prayer was more for those who were listening and watching than for Himself. "Then Jesus looked up and said, Father, I thank you that you have heard me. I knew that you always hear me, but I said this for the benefit of the people standing here, that they may believe that you sent me."[1] Then He called the man by name who had been dead and buried for four days, and Lazarus came back to life.

Once a person understands what the Father has already given and accepts all of its benefits by faith, the response is praise and thanksgiving. Jesus' prayer models that. He thanked His Father that He always heard Him. In fact, He said that He "heard" him. Nothing had yet happened but Jesus had already discussed the matter with His Father and He was confident that He had been heard and His Father would respond. How was He so sure? It was because of His faith that had been tested by trial and previous experience.

The prophet wrote, "My people are destroyed for lack of knowledge."[2] If one has no knowledge of what is available freely through Jesus, is misinformed about these things or even willingly ignorant, there is no confidence, thereby making praise and thanksgiving difficult, nearly impossible.

---

[1] John 11:41-42

[2] Hosea 4:6

Faith is Not in What is Seen

For some, faith is about seeing things: financial prosperity in millions of dollars, luxury cars and palatial homes without any sickness or trouble. If those things are not manifested, some have difficulty praising God. In these instances praise is connected to visible outcomes and manifestations. Some say, when things are going well in life—home, job, and finances, they can praise God. If I just bought a new car, or had a false alarm regarding a serious illness, I can praise Him.

When, however, praise flows from an understanding of what God has given in Christ, circumstances are irrelevant and the character of that believer's praise is different. It is what the Bible calls, "the sacrifice of praise."[3] The prophet Habakkuk put it this way:

> Though the fig tree does not bud
> and there are no grapes on the vines,
> though the olive crop fails
> and the fields produce no food,
> though there are no sheep in the pen
> and no cattle in the stalls,
> yet I will rejoice in the LORD,
> I will be joyful in God my Savior.[4]

Jesus and the Apostles had difficulties, pressures, troubles, persecutions, hardships, lack and hunger. Their faith was not based on the things that could be seen. It was focused on He who is invisible. It was based on what God had declared in His Word. And their prayers were full of praise and thanksgiving. Here is a sample of some of Paul's recorded prayers:

---

[3] Hebrews 13:15

[4] Habakkuk 3:17-18

Praise be to the God and Father of our Lord Jesus Christ, who blessed us in the heavenly realms with every spiritual blessing in Christ. For he chose us in him before the creation of the world to be holy and blameless in his sight. In love he predestined us to be adopted as his son through Jesus Christ, in accordance with his pleasure and will-to the praise of his glorious grace, which he has freely given us in the One he loves. In him we have redemption through his blood, the forgiveness of sins, in accordance with the riches of God's grace that he lavished on us with all wisdom and understanding. And he made known to us the mystery of his will according to his good pleasure, which he purposed in Christ, to be put into effect when the times will have reached their fulfillment-to bring all things in heaven and on earth together under one head, even Christ.

I keep asking that the God of our Lord Jesus Christ, the glorious Father, may give you the Spirit of wisdom and revelation, so that you may know You better. I pray also that the eyes of your heart may be enlightened in order that you may know the hope to which he has called you, the riches of his glorious inheritance in the saints, and his incomparably great power for us who believe. That power is like the working of his mighty strength, which he exerted in Christ when he raised him from the dead and seated him at his right hand in the heavenly realms, far above all rule and authority, power and dominion, and every title that can be given, not only in the present age but also in the one to come. And You placed all things under his feet and appointed him to be head over everything for the church, which is his body, the fullness of him who fills everything in every way.

I pray that out of his glorious riches he may strengthen you with power through his Spirit in your inner being, so that Christ may dwell in your hearts through faith. And I pray that you, being rooted and established in love, may have power, together with all the saints, to grasp how wide and long and high and deep is the love of Christ, and to know this love that surpasses knowledge-that I may be filled to the measure of all the fullness of God.

Now to him who is able to do immeasurably more than all we ask or imagine, according to his power that is at work within us, to him be glory in the church and in Christ Jesus throughout all generations, for ever and ever! Amen.

And this is my prayer: that your love may abound more and more in knowledge and depth of insight, so that you may be able to discern what is best and may be pure and blameless until the day of Christ, filled with the fruit of righteousness that comes through Jesus Christ-to the glory and praise of God.

...I have not stopped praying and asking God to fill you with the knowledge of his will through all spiritual wisdom and understanding. And we pray this in order that you may live a life worthy of the Lord and may please him in every way: bearing fruit in every good work, growing in the knowledge of God, being strengthened with all power according to his glorious might so that you may have great endurance and patience, and joyfully giving thanks to the Father, who has qualified you to share in the inheritance of the

> *saints in the kingdom of light. For he has rescued me from the dominion of darkness and brought me into the kingdom of the Son he loves, in whom we have redemption, the forgiveness of sins.*[5]

Praise is an expression of the believer's trust in God's willingness and ability to do what He said he has done and what He will do. It is specific and informed in what God is being praised and thanked for. This is what makes the study of the word so essential. Ultimately, prayers are reminding and thanking God for what He said He has done and will do.

Prayers are reminding and thanking God for what He said He has done and will do

Confession

First, one must believe it in his heart, then confession is made with the mouth.[6] To confess means to say what one believes.[7] When the believer speaks in agreement with what God says, he is making his confession regarding that thing. When a believer confesses one's sin he is in agreement with God with regard to that particular transgression. There is also the positive confession by agreeing with what God has declared regarding the believer. The believer believes, so he speaks what is believed.

Praise and thanksgiving are related to confession. To praise someone means to boast or brag about that person

[5] From The Power Prayer Scepter Communications Lake Monroe FL 2006. Adapted from Ephesians 1:3-10, 17-23, 3:16-21, Philippians 1:9-10 and Colossians 1:9b-14.

[6] Romans 10:9

[7] NIV Bible Dictionary Concordance Bible Study Helps Zondervan Grand Rapids, MI 1984

to someone else. It is to commend, to applaud, and to extol in word or song. Praise fills the atmosphere of the life of the believer who now has believed and received what the Father has freely given in Christ. When one lifts up praise to Christ, essentially he is agreeing with or confessing the Father's revelation regarding His Son. Even in the midst of adverse circumstances, praise and thanksgiving flow forth freely.

Paul urged the believers in Phillipi to rejoice in the Lord always.[8] Even while incarcerated in prison, praise is echoed throughout the cellblocks. As ferocious beasts prepared to tear believers apart during the persecution in Rome, they sang their praises to the Father.[9]

The corporate worship of believers who have received the Father's gift is filled with praise. Unbelievers who have not experienced or accepted the Gift of God observe and are drawn to Him. As His praise is proclaimed, sinners and unbelievers will inquire and themselves become believers.[10]

The life of a believer becomes a life of praise. Sharing what God has freely given with friends and neighbors is like finding something valuable and out of excitement sharing it with friends. Out of an intense sense of gratitude one serves and is eager to please the Giver of the Gift. Love overflows from the heart and there is nothing too extravagant that we can do for Him.

---

[8] Philippians 4:4

[9] See Foxes Book of Christian Martyrs by John Foxe, Whitaker House, New Kensington, PA 1988

[10] Psalm 51:12-13

The Tabernacle of David

The apostle James, responding to a dispute about the entrance of gentiles into the body of believers, cites a prophecy by Amos about the "tabernacle of David." While the primary focus of the passage was about the restoration of the throne of David by God's anointed Son, the specific characteristics of David's tabernacle cannot be overlooked. The Temples of the wilderness, Solomon's, Zerubabel's and Herod's, each of which were different from David's Tabernacle, were not mentioned as a model of this future temple of praise.

David's tent had no compartments. There was no holy or most holy place. It was simply a tent that housed the ark which was a symbol of the presence of God. Its services involved evening and morning sacrifices as well as other activities as prescribed in the books of Moses.

Its most dominant feature, however, as recorded in scripture, was its focus on praising God continually. Specific priests were assigned to sing and perform on instruments to accompany the glorifying of God. This was the priority for David's tabernacle.

David learned to praise God as a boy alone with his father's sheep, in the court of Saul, and in the wilderness in trouble and on the run. When his reign was at its height and he had rest from all of his enemies, he brought the ark, signifying the presence of God, to Jerusalem. Now, as king, he did what he had done in the worst of times and in the best of times; he praised the God of his salvation.

Prophetically, James declared that God will rebuild David's fallen tent and that will also include the primary characteristic of praise and worship.

Praise in Heaven

John was given a glimpse into the atmosphere of praise in Heaven. It was loud. It was ecstatic. It was non-stop and ongoing. Every being there was involved. And, for those in the earth who have received the gift freely given by the Father, their praise on earth will merge with and begin to resemble that of Heaven.

Paul exclaimed, "Thanks be to God for his indescribable Gift!" The more closely one looks, the more amazing He is, and the more grateful and thankful one will become. He is worthy and greatly to be praised. Let heaven and earth proclaim it. As David penned in song after song, God the Father is my Savior and Deliverer and if I had a million tongues I could not tell it all.

He sent His Son and through and with Him I was crucified, died, was buried, quickened by His Spirit, raised to live a new life, seated with Him on His Father's right hand and glorified. He is my wisdom, righteousness, justification, sanctification, and glorification.[11] This was the Father's desire and will. He is to be praised and thanked.

Paul asks as he concludes, "What shall we say to these things?

> *If God is for us, who can be against us? He who did not spare his own Son, but gave him up for us all—how will he not also, along with him, graciously give us all things? Who will bring any charge against those whom God has chosen? It is God who justifies. Who is he that condemns? Christ Jesus, who died—more than that, who was raised to life—is at the right hand of God and is also interceding for us. Who shall separate us from the love of Christ? Shall trouble or hardship*

[11] 1 Corinthians 1:30

> *or persecution or famine or nakedness or danger or sword? As it is written: "For your sake we face death all day long; we are considered as sheep to be slaughtered." No, in all these things we are more than conquerors through him who loved us. For I am convinced that neither death nor life, neither angels nor demons, neither the present nor the future, nor any powers, neither height nor depth, nor anything else in all creation, will be able to separate us from the love of God that is in Christ Jesus our Lord*[12]

There is only one response, and that response is experienced with all of our being (spirit, soul and body). To God be the Glory! Thanks be to God for His indescribable Gift.

---

[12] Romans 8:31-39

Appendix

Suggested Reading

These are only a few of the many writers and their works that reinforced what the Spirit of God revealed in the scriptures. Use this brief list as a starting point to augment your study in the Word of God.

Bevere, John

The Fear of the Lord (Lake Mary, Florida: Strang Communications, 1997)

Under Cover: Your Secret Place of Freedom (Nashville, Tennessee: Thomas Nelson, 2001)

Foxe, John

Foxe's Book of Christian Martyrs (New Kensington, Pennsylvania: Whitaker House, 1985)

Hamon, Bill

Prophets and Personal Prophecy (New Kensington, Pennsylvania: Destiny Image, 1987)

Prophets, Pitfalls and Principles (New Kensington, Pennsylvania: Destiny Image, 1990)

Prophets and the Prophetic Movement (New Kensington, Pennsylvania: Destiny Image, 1991)

Jacobs, Cindy

The Voice of God (Ventura, California: Gospel Light, 1997)

Meyer, Joyce

The Battlefield of the Mind (New York, New York: Time Warner Book Group, 1999)

MUNROE, MYLES

The Power and Purpose of Praise and Worship (New Kensington, Pennsylvania: Destiny Image, 2000)

The Power and Purpose of Prayer (New Kensington, Pennsylvania: Destiny Image, 2002)

Understanding the Power and Purpose of Men (New Kensington, Pennsylvania: Destiny Image, 2001)

Understanding the Power and Purpose of Women (New Kensington, Pennsylvania: Destiny Image, 2001)

NEE, WATCHMAN

The Normal Christian Life (Wheaton, Illinois: Tyndale House, 1997)

Sit, Stand, Walk (Anaheim, California: Living Stream Ministry, 1997)

The Breaking of the Outer Man (Anaheim, California: Living Stream Ministry, 1997)

Authority and Submission (Anaheim, California: Living Stream Ministry, 1998)

The Spiritual Man (Anaheim, California: Living Stream Ministry, 1998)

The Ministry of God's Word (Anaheim, California: Living Stream Ministry, 2000)

The Ministry of Christ (Anaheim, California: Living Stream Ministry, 1997)

SORGE, BOB

Exploring Worship (Central Point, Oregon: Oasis House, 1987)

WHITT, MARCOS

A Worship Filled Life (Lake Mary Florida: Strang Communications, 1998)

About the Author

For over twenty years Pastor S.L. Walters has been involved in ministry as a practicing Pastor and Evangelist. His ministry has brought him to almost every major city on the east coast and elsewhere including:

Albany, NY
Hyde Park, NY
Hempstead, NY
New York, NY
Boston, MA
Springfield, MA
Hartford, CT
Bloomfield, CT
New Haven, CT
Newark, NJ
Philadelphia, PA
Baltimore, MD
Washington, DC
Asheville, NC
Augusta, GA
Atlanta, GA
Decatur, GA
Tifton, GA
Fitzgerald, GA
Orlando, FL
Flint, MI
New Orleans, LA
Fort Worth, TX
Houston, TX
Inglewood, CA
Cassopolis, MI
Berrien Springs, MI
Saint Joseph, MI
Benton Harbor, MI
Rochester, NY
Winter Park, FL
Spartanburg, SC
Pompano Beach, FL
Fort Lauderdale, FL
Dania, FL
Hollywood, FL
Miami, FL
Coconut Grove, FL
Huntsville, AL
Harvest, AL
Birmingham, AL
Montgomery, AL
Shreveport, LA
Minden, LA
Mansfield, LA
Metairie, LA
Hammond, LA
Lansing, MI
Chicago, IL
Grand Rapids, MI
Brooklyn, NY
Staten Island, NY

Pastor Walters has formal training in Religion and Broadcast Communications with BA and MDiv Degrees from Oakwood University in Huntsville, Alabama and Andrews University in Berrien Springs, Michigan respectively. He also has done his doctoral studies at United Theological Seminary in Dayton Ohio. He has practical experience in broadcast media in the areas of:

Production Assistant

Camera Operator

Film and Slide Chain Operator

Audio Engineer and Designer

Technical Director

Film Editor and Librarian

Radio Announcer

Free - Lance Producer / Director

Now Pastor Walters' only focus is to teach, preach and promote the Gospel of the kingdom of God and His Christ under the leadership and direction of the Spirit of God through the activities of Answer Ministries International Inc. and its affiliated ministries. www.amiintl.org.

NOTES

NOTES

NOTES

www.ingramcontent.com/pod-product-compliance
Lightning Source LLC
LaVergne TN
LVHW091153080426
835509LV00006B/672

9780983546405